Retire with Abundance

Learn How to Take the Struggle Out of the Climb

By
Matthew Dworetsky

The Top Advisors
Starting Point Publishing
1401 Hemlock Ave.
Nashville, TN 37216
Phone: 734-545-0900

ISBN 978-1-6929-487-33

Printed in the United States of America.

Additional copies may be available at special discounts for bulk purchase in the U.S. for church groups, corporations, Institutions, and other organizations. For more information please contact: Phone: 734-545-0900.

This book is printed on acid-free paper. It meets or exceeds the guidelines for permanence and durability of the Committee on Production Guidelines for Book Longevity of the Council on Library Resources.

Table of Contents

Retire with Abundance

CHAPTER 1

Inflation, Taxes and...

We are facing many problems in the United States as we write this book. We're concerned these obstacles may not be corrected or overcome. We hope we are wrong. Stick with us and you will see why we are concerned about the near future financially.

Our Nation, as of this printing, is 31 trillion dollars in debt. As of this writing, we are spending 6.2 trillion dollars and our nation's income as of this printing was 4.8 trillion. The difference is called the "*deficit*." We are spending close to 1.2 trillion more than we make as a country! On top of that we owe 1.5 trillion for Medicare and Medicaid, 1.1 trillion for Social Security and over spending 700 billion on defense. The grand total if you add all the above together is 41 trillion dollars between debt and overspending.

For many, hearing these numbers has become so common, that after a while we don't even know what it means. We hear millions, billions, and trillions, but do we really understand how much we are talking about or does it all kind of mesh together after a while?

First let's look at the numbers.

One million dollars looks like this: $1,000,000.
One billion dollars looks like this: $1,000,000,000.
One trillion dollars looks like this: $1,000,000,000,000

"Okay", you say, "that looks right. So what?"

Look at your wristwatch or a clock, and then ask yourself *how long is a trillion seconds?*

The answer is 32,000 YEARS!!! Now multiply 32,000 years times 41 and that is how much money our country is in debt when looked at in years using seconds.

PHEW!

The Federal Reserve is responsible for printing US currency not the Treasury Department. Whenever the U.S. doesn't sell enough of their bonds to get the income (above and beyond other streams of income they depend on (i.e., taxes) then they ask the Federal Reserve to print enough money for them to buy their own bonds.

This would be like you running short of income in one year and just running down to your basement or garage and printing the rest of the money you need. Would you ever worry about a budget or controlling your spending? The answer is most assuredly NO!

Here is an article I found on the printing of money and what it can mean from CNBC.com. I have not printed the entire article for sake of space. Should you wish to read the article you again can find it on www.cnbc.com.

Fed analysis warns of 'economic ruin' when governments print money to pay off debt

Published Mon, Nov 25 2019 12:29 Pm Est
updated Tue, Nov 26 2019 1:28 Pm Est

> Federal Reserve economists warn that printing money to pay for deficit spending has been a disaster for other nations that have tried it.
>
> In a paper that discusses the burgeoning U.S. fiscal debt, Fed experts note that high levels are not necessarily unsustainable so long as income is rising at a faster pace. They note that countries that have gotten into trouble and looked to central banks to bail them out haven't fared well.

"A solution some countries with high levels of unsustainable debt have tried is printing money. In this scenario, the government borrows money by issuing bonds and then orders the central bank to buy those bonds by creating (printing) money," wrote Scott A. Wolla and Kaitlyn Frerking. "History has taught us, however, that this type of policy leads to extremely high rates of inflation (hyperinflation) and often ends in economic ruin."

Having read this the question then is just how much money is the Federal Reserve Printing so the U.S can buy its own bonds to *just cover the annual deficit* (not the total debt)? Here is what I found.

2020 Federal Reserve Note Print Order

The Board of Governors (the Board), as the issuing authority for Federal Reserve notes, approved and submitted its fiscal year (FY) 2020 order for approximately 5.2 billion Federal Reserve notes, valued at $146.4 billion, to the U.S. Treasury Department's Bureau of Engraving and Printing (BEP) on August 6, 2019.1

The 5.2 billion notes included in the FY 2020 order reflect the Board's estimate of net demand for currency from domestic and international customers. The print order is determined by denomination and is based on destruction rates and historical payments to and receipts from circulation. As in past years, the primary purpose of the print order is to replace the unfit notes that the Reserve Banks will destroy during normal processing of notes returned from circulation.2 Other factors include a planned inventory adjustment, estimates of net payments, and a contingency for international demand variability. The table below reflects the denominational breakdown of the Boards' FY 2020 order.3

https://www.federalreserve.gov/paymentsystems/coin_currency_orders.htm

According to the Committee for a Responsible Federal Budget (*www.crfb.org*):

- **Debt is Rising Unsustainably**. Under current law, CBO projects federal debt held by the public will rise from 80 percent of GDP this year to 144 percent by 2049—more than a third higher than the historic record of 106 percent set just after World War II.

- **Spending is Growing Faster than Revenue.** CBO projects spending will grow rapidly, from less than 21 percent of GDP in 2019 to over 28 percent by 2049. Revenue will grow more slowly, from 16.5 percent of GDP this year to 19.5 percent by 2049. As a result, annual deficits are expected to more than double from 4.2 percent of GDP in 2019 to 8.7 percent by 2049.

According to *www.usgovernmentspending.com*, over the three years 2013 to 2015, our country was averaging an annual budget deficit of:

500 billion dollars per year.

That looks like this:

$500,000,000,000

Today the deficit for 2022 is over 2.6 trillion dollars that we are in debt as a country over what we take in. That looks like this:

$2,000,000,000,000 (*https://www.usdebtclock.org 4/17/2020*)

Government spending is at 6.2 trillion for this year. For one year! (*usdebtclock.org 4/17/2020*).

In addition, the scale of U.S. government money creation is staggering: Eight days ago, the central bank announced $700 billion in bond purchases (*https://www.nytimes.com/2020/03/23/upshot/coronavirus-fed-extraordinary-response.html*). Now it is saying that could be higher, plausibly in the trillions of dollars. This means the US government can't sell enough of their bonds to pay their bills so the Fed's just up and print more money and use the new money to buy the bonds, so the US doesn't go into bankruptcy.

As of this writing, we are in the middle of a pandemic with the Corona Virus. Questions:

- How will the government already overspending more than they take in possibly cover the trillions in bailouts they are creating for those impacted by the Coronavirus in 2020?

- How can we afford more debt, now looking at 25 trillion once the bailouts are completed?

As more businesses go under, that means less tax revenue to a system that is already running on a thin thread.

- With more businesses going under, unemployment is hitting levels like the 1929 crash and we are even done yet. What happens with all the lost tax revenues from those who no longer are working?

Total debt to GDP (Gross Domestic Product / us income) is now at 128.4% and the *debt per taxpayer* in America now stands at **$195,945. How many people in America have a spare $200,000 sitting around?** (*usdebtclock.org 4/17/2020*).

Current US Federal Government Spending
How Does Congress Really Spend YOUR Money?
Why Spending Is Increasing

Before the recession the government kept federal spending below 20% of GDP. It grew no faster than the economy, around 2% to 3% per year. During the recession, spending grew to a record 24.4% of GDP in Fiscal Year 2009. This increase was due to economic stimulus and two overseas wars.

At the same time, growth slowed. That reduced tax receipts. Congress worried about the ballooning U.S. debt. No one could agree on how to reduce it. As a result, Congress enacted a 10%

budget cut, called sequestration that finally reduced spending to 20.7% of GDP in FY 2015.

Since then, spending has crept up again despite the sequester. Congress and the president rely on deficit spending to boost economic growth.

But deficit spending is out of control. It rises each year even when the economy is doing well. A **Deficit** is the amount our government spends over and above what it takes in. Debt would represent the total accumulation of deficits over the years. In addition, if you count our "unfunded obligations" (commitments we have made as a nation to entitlement programs like Medicare and Social Security), *www.usdebtclock.org* reveals the eye-popping numbers putting the overall figure of debt (including unfunded liabilities) at an astonishing $168.8 trillion dollars. If 1 trillion seconds is about 32,000 years and we have $168.8 trillion in debt, I'll let you do the math.

I hope and pray for the sake of our country and our children's future that Congress will wake up to finally put the country ahead of special interest groups and wasteful spending. I have never understood how basic household accounting says always spend less than what you earn, and yet some of our nations seemingly brightest people can't get it under control. I have my theories as to why, but I will keep that to myself for now.

Let's get back to the issue of printing money. What does it hurt for the Federal Reserve to print more money if they believe it will help the country? My answer is that they are affixing a bandage on an open wound.

There is only so much U.S. currency floating around the world at any one time and our dollar is given a value in comparison to other currencies based on the strength of our economy and other factors. If the Federal Reserve prints more money and adds it to the circulation of existing dollars, then each dollar already in circulation is valued less. Printing more money negatively impacts the current value of existing dollars.

Let me give you an example. If the U.S. doubles the amount of U.S. dollars floating around the world, the added dollars then makes each dollar worth less. If I had a one-of-a-kind rare painting it can have a high worth. However, if I discover there were two others just like it, the one I own is now worth less. The same holds true when the Federal Reserve prints more money. If they were to double the amount of American dollars in the world then the existing dollars lose value just like the painting. Each dollar is not as valuable as they once were. Let's assume the manufacturer of a pen or writing instrument has been selling pens for one dollar, and by doing so can profit 50 cents. Now assume the Federal Reserve prints enough new money to effectively double the amount of U.S. dollars circulating in the world. This makes each dollar now only worth 50 cents. The pen manufacturer must now raise their price to two dollars in order to make the same profit as before as each dollar they collect for the pen is now worth only 50 cents.

What is this called when everything goes up in price? INFLATION. I have read many articles touting both sides of the potential of coming inflation. On one side many claim due to the printing of money inflation is all but certain. The other side says that in order to have inflation we must have demand for goods and services in order to drive up prices. As of the writing of this book, the U.S. economy didn't create enough demand as many families and individuals are fighting just to make ends meet. I decided to look back in history for my answer and to formulate my own opinion.

From 1979 to 1980 when Jimmy Carter was President, we went through one of the worst inflation eras in U.S. history. According to www.inflationdata.com, inflation rose over those two years by a combined 24.8%. If it had stayed that high, the cost of things we buy would double every 5.8 years (using the rule of 72 which says divide 72 by the rate and the result is how long it takes to double). So, what was the demand back then? Were we full of prosperity? No! By the end of 1982 the unemployment rate reached 10.4% (*www.multpl.com*)!

Prior to the Corona Virus hitting, we were at one of the lowest unemployment rates in history for every part of society. Now as of April 17, 2020, we have 22 million unemployed and that equates out to about 6.6% unemployment.

So, demand for goods and services should slow considerably. While demand can be a condition for inflation, in my opinion it is only one path to inflation. The other is the printing of money and the devaluing of the dollar which is what we are seeing today and seeing it in amounts never seen in history. I believe the massive printing of money that the Federal Reserve Board is printing today will result in more inflation eventually. Later, I will discuss things you can be doing to prepare and hedge against this coming epidemic. By the way, I am not just talking about gold.

As you join me in reading the chapters that follow, I know you will find some answers you have been seeking in how to better manage your investments, finances, and retirement dreams in light of these facts and the economy we find ourselves in.

I also hope and pray our government will learn to manage their spending and debt. That's one that I believe only prayer can resolve. Many say it would be a miracle...From 1979 to 1980, when Jimmy Carter was President, we went through one of the worst inflation eras in U.S. history. According to *www.inflationdata. com*, inflation rose over those two years by a combined 24.8%. If it had stayed that high, the cost of things we buy would double every 5.8 years (using the rule of 72 which says divide 72 by the rate and the result is how long it takes to double). So what was the demand back then? Were we full of prosperity? No! By the end of 1982 the unemployment rate reached 10.4% (*www.multpl.com*)!

Prior to the Corona Virus hitting, we were at one of the lowest unemployment rates in history for every part of society. Now as of April 17, 2020, we have 22 million unemployed and that equates out to about 6.6% unemployment.

So, demand for goods and services should slow considerably. While demand can be a condition for inflation, in my opinion it is only one path to inflation. The other is the printing of money and the devaluing of the dollar which is what we are seeing today, and seeing it in amounts never before seen in history. I believe the massive printing of money that the Federal Reserve Board is printing today will result in more inflation eventually. Later, I will discuss things you can be doing to prepare and hedge against this coming epidemic. By the way, I am not just talking about gold.

As you join me in reading the chapters that follow, I know you will find some answers you have been seeking in how to better manage your investments, finances, and retirement dreams in light of these facts and the economy we find ourselves in.

I also hope and pray our government will learn to manage their spending and debt. That's one that I believe only prayer can resolve. Many say it would be a miracle...

CHAPTER 2

What is it You Want?

Is retirement just around the corner for you, or are you are already there? Like most people, your goal is to have a successful and secure retirement. You want a retirement where you will never run out of income and can have the financial freedom to enjoy your life after work. Why, for many, does this seem so hard to achieve? Why does this create fear of the actual capability of achieving the retirement they have dreamed of? I will be addressing these and many more questions as we share time together. I will share with you what your financial advisor has failed to tell you that puts your retirement at risk. I will share a strategy that puts you back in control of your future.

It never ceases to amaze me how many new people come into our offices and are shocked by how much risk they are carrying in their investment portfolios. The number one reason for this is that your advisor has failed to communicate with you on a level you can understand. With the strategies in this book, you will once and for all learn how to communicate to your advisor what you do and don't want, and you'll forever be in control of how your money is invested.

If you will bear with me, I would like to start by going back to the beginning stages of designing the retirement you want. For many who deal mostly with a large broker/dealer, these critical steps are missed. Therefore, allow me to take you there. It really is the critical first step!

I once heard a person say that he could shoot the apple off another person's head better than the famed archer William Tell. That is provided you blindfolded William Tell, spun him around five times and pointed him in the wrong direction. You say "That's crazy! How can he hit a target he cannot see?" That's exactly my point! How can you achieve a retirement when you have no idea what you want or what it looks like?

What is it that you want? This can actually be looked at from two angles. What you do want and what don't you want. From all of my years in counseling retirees, here are the most popular responses for what we want: freedom to travel, visit relatives, have good health, and give back.

Freedom to Travel

Did you ever see the movie *The Bucket List*? It stars Jack Nicholson and Morgan Freeman. I found it to be very entertaining. Yet most important, it helps us see how we can sometimes be so busy in life that we never stop to dream and think about what it is we really want to do or accomplish before we pass away.

For many, retirement means the ability to travel. It's important for you to talk to your spouse or get with a friend and break out a pad of paper and begin to dream. Make your own "bucket list" of things you want to do and places you would like to go during your retirement years. Where are some of the places in the world or this country you have always wanted to visit but have never been? Within America, how about Niagara Falls? Go and hear the roar of the water. Take the cruise up to the base of the Falls.

How about staying in a Bed and Breakfast in the New England states during autumn and enjoy the changing of the leaves to the reds, orange and yellow colors that can take your breath away. You could visit the Grand Canyon and ride the mules or if health allows ride the rapids of the Colorado River. You might want to see the Redwood Forest of California where the size and majesty of the trees cannot be explained. There are many other options like cruising the Smoky Mountains in a convertible, going to Disneyland, or Alaska.

When you think of the World, have you ever wanted to visit the British Isles and see the amazing green of Ireland or the streets of London? How about touring Europe to see the Eiffel Tower in Paris, the Swiss Alps, or the streets of Italy? You could visit the Far East or Australia? What would you do if you could? Dream… make your bucket list today! Don't put it off!

Ability to Visit Kids and Grandkids

For some this is easy as they live close. For others it is much harder. My wife and I have friends whose children live in China and other friends whose children live in Alaska. That could mean fewer visits. However, no matter where our children and grandchildren live, visiting them is typically a major goal or want. How often would you like to see your grandchildren? What would it take?

Have Good Health

Aging usually comes with our bodies breaking down over time. While it is inevitable that we will all someday die, we want to enjoy the best health possible along the way. Affording great health care is a key for most people in retirement. Paint a picture of what your health will be like over the first 10 years of retirement. Remember, you can't hit a target you can't see, even if it is in your mind!

Giving Back

For some the idea of giving back in a financial way or by giving of our time is critical. One of my clients for years volunteered for the American Red Cross. He got to see parts of the world he would otherwise never have seen. While it wasn't under the ideal circumstances, he spent many years serving others and touching lives. Do you have a charitable heart? Have you spent your life caring for your family, and are now looking to invest in the lives of others? I don't believe we should aspire to retire and do nothing. We should always long to retire to do something with the years we have left. The question is what is the something you plan to retire to?

Over the years, one common thing shared by all of my clients is that they constantly tell me how busy life is in retirement. It's not uncommon to hear them say, "I don't know how I ever had time for a job before. I seem to run from the time I get up until the time I go to bed." So you see, we all retire to something other than just lying around. Again, it's up to you to set the priorities of what you will be retiring to do. If left undetermined, vacant time never stays vacant. If you don't make the decision of how your time is filled, someone or something else will.

Again, from all my years of counseling, here are the most popular responses for what my clients do not want; to rely on children financially or physically, to run out of money, have an estate go through probate, or overpay on taxes.

Reliance on Our Kids Financially or Physically

No one wants to be dependent on financial help from their children. Therefore, proper planning and securing your retirement can make sure this never happens. While physically there is only so much we can do to remain independent, again the proper finances can mean never being a burden to our children.

To Run Out of Money

Financial security is one of the chief goals of every retiree. Not being able to pay our bills can be one of our main concerns. Not being able to afford a certain level of lifestyle can make for a long and frustrating 20 to 30 years in retirement. Later, I will share strategies that can help guarantee you will never run out of income for the rest of your life.

Have Estate Go Through Probate

In some states probate is easier than others. However, in most cases it is far better to avoid probate if for no other reason than the privacy issues a trust can provide. There are many who think the best idea is to put your child's name on your bank and investment accounts or the title to your home. THIS CAN BE A VERY DANGEROUS MISTAKE! Later we will teach you the pros and cons of why, as well as the pros and cons of a Trust versus a Will.

To Overpay Our Taxes

There is never a time when reducing our taxes is more important than in our retirement years. The less we pay in taxes, the more income we have in retirement and the longer our invested assets will last. I am not saying we should not support our government financially. I am an advocate of only sharing with the government that which we legally owe. As long as we are following the law when we figure our taxes, and do so legally, it is only appropriate that our money last our lifetime.

For many, they believe reducing taxes in our highest earning years is critical. However, seldom do taxes destroy our livelihood while we are working. Yet in retirement, reportable taxable income can make the difference in an enjoyable retirement versus a retirement in which we struggle to make ends meet. Your Social Security Income could be tax free if you handle your income properly in retirement. Unfortunately it is a rare advisor indeed who counsels a client in this regard. Usually it is simply investment advice **not "income" advice.** I'm truly looking forward to discussing this later in some detail to help you achieve the highest possible income with the lowest possible tax.

Let me tell you a story about Bob and Ruth (I changed their names to protect their anonymity). When Bob and Ruth came to see me in 2004, Bob was a retired barber and Ruth was a homemaker. As you might guess barbers don't have a pension plan, so Bob and Ruth were living off of their combined Social Security which amounted to about $25,000 per year. In addition, they were utilizing some of their investments. The total amount of income they needed per year was $43,000 of which $25,000 was coming from Social Security and $18,000 from their investment portfolio. When Bob and Ruth first came to see me, I noticed that their investments were actually in pretty good shape. However, where they or their advisor had failed involved how they took their income and therefore paid their taxes. I suggested that we make a phone call together. We called one of their investment companies and I asked them to change one thing about their account. **We tweaked one thing and their taxes fell to zero.** They still had the same $43,000 in income, but they stopped paying any tax on the interest income and Social Security income. All because of one simple phone call. You see, it took a while but we had to help Bob and Ruth figure out what they needed and what they wanted. Once they realized they needed the entire $43,000 free of tax and got the proper advice, this was accomplished.

Have you ever heard the phrase "When a student is ready, the teacher will appear?" Bob and Ruth were ready. They couldn't make ends meet by paying taxes on their income. Bob and Ruth didn't care about stocks, bonds, mutual funds, or annuities. What they cared about was getting the income they needed and securing it for life. It's a great deal of fun to see them for their annual review each year. I ask them the same question. "How much did you pay in taxes last year?" Bob looks at me and gets a big old grin on his face and says… "Nothing!"

The first step is to determine at what age you would like to retire. The second step is to identify how much income you need in order to have the lifestyle you desire and determine what portfolio balance is required to provide that income. Keep in mind that you will need to adjust for inflation throughout your retirement years. Otherwise, you end up sliding toward poverty with each year you live.

Over the last 30 years, one of the most common things I have run into in the financial services business is when I start off by talking to someone and asking them a very profound question, at what age do they plan to retire. Mind you my clients are mostly over the age of 50 and those who are still working have a hard time coming up with an answer. The husband may look at his wife and say, "Gee, honey, I don't know. I've never really thought about it. What do you think?" The wife looks back at her husband and says, "You're the one who handles the money (or vice versa) what do you think?" The husband says, "I just pay the bills not plan our retirement." This can go on for quite some time before they both finally come up with an age they *think* they would like to retire. Then with a sheepish look on their faces, they look over at me and answer with a question rather than an exclamation point or period as they say, "65?"

The truth is most couples have seldom talked about it nor have single people thought about it. They each may have fantasized in their own minds when that day may be. However, they've spent more time planning their last vacation than they did talking about the day they plan to retire, which could easily be a 30-year plan or more not just a 7-day vacation.

Assuming you are already in retirement or have now come up with the age you plan to retire, as stated earlier, the next step would be to identify how much income you will need. For many couples, they have never even put together a household budget for today much less plan their income needs after they retire. You see there are so many things to think about surrounding ones retirement that they fail to understand the importance of professional help in planning this major event that in today's world could last 30 years or more.

This book is not being written with the objective of helping you identify your annual budget in retirement. A rule of thumb is that you will need approximately 80% of the income you had before you retire. Making a commitment one evening to sit down and put what you are spending on paper will pay off handsomely for your future. Make it a date. Go out for a nice dinner and then come home and start writing down your bills and payments. I think you will be surprised by how little time it will take. There are many good books on the market that delve into the subject of budgeting. I will leave each reader to their own to work out the details and the amount of income you will need for your retirement. The key is to at least identify some amount of income it would take to give you the retirement lifestyle you seek.

Once you identify the income needed, you must now focus on what amount of money you must have in your investment portfolio in order to draw the income you desire or need. Once that is determined, you then must factor in inflation. You cannot simply say, "I need $50,000 per year in addition to Social Security to have the income I need. With 5% interest calculated, I'll need one million dollars." If you retired this way, you would slowly be slipping into poverty. You must plan for inflation and also look for inflation hedges for the years that inflation accelerates beyond its average of 3 to 4% over time. If this last paragraph leaves you confused, I don't blame you. However, hang in there as later when we get to investment strategies, I will be discussing some investment vehicles that will help you when these times appear.

I once had a single lady who came in for her first visit with me. She was living on $30,000 per year and had over one million in her investment portfolio. When I asked her why she was struggling on so little income while having a sizable investment portfolio with which to support her needs, her answer was the same as many who have since followed her. She said, "I am afraid I may someday run out of money and therefore want to use as little as possible, just in case."

I am concerned by how many people have the "cross my fingers" approach to their retirement. They have no idea what they can and can't afford to do in retirement. Some live like paupers on as little as possible for fear they will run out. Others live above their means and are on a one-way ticket to financial disaster and don't know it.

In this book, I will teach you how to manage your money so that you will always be in charge of your financial life. I will teach you how to, in as little as 30 minutes **each year, *know exactly*** where you stand. You will know how much you can afford to spend each year. You will know if you are ahead of the curve, right on track or behind.

I will teach you investment strategies that will help you get what you want, avoid what you don't want and never be totally at the mercy of a financial advisor for proper decision making again. Please don't misunderstand me. I believe to do things right, a qualified advisor can be critical and well worth their time and fee. However, too many retirees put their entire faith in the advisor (be it a CPA, CFP, CWS, or any other financial advisor) and really don't have any idea if the advisor is doing what they have asked them to do or if the advisor is doing what he or she wants or thinks is right. A professional advisor is not there to do what they think is right or wrong. They are in your life to educate you, give you the pros and cons of your options, and guide you in achieving YOUR goals not theirs. A professional financial advisor is like an architect who is there to help you design your retirement according to your specifications.

You must have a plan in retirement. Without one, you are "unemployed!" Let's look at it another way. If you were 45 and suddenly lost your job, how would you react? Would there be panic? I imagine one of the first things to cross your mind would be how will I pay my bills? How will we make the mortgage payment? What about our cars? Losing one's job can be one of the most financially traumatic events we can face.

Not having a planned and structured retirement is really the same thing. Without a retirement plan, how will you pay your mortgage? How will you buy your groceries? The questions can be the same. Yet for some reason, most of us don't even stop to think about the retirement issue seriously enough until it's too late to do anything to correct it.

This book is not being written with the idea of teaching younger adults how to build their retirement. It is being written with two objectives in mind.

First, if you are behind financially on planning for your retirement, is there anything you can do to catch up? Let's say you are 55 and want to retire at 65. To get the income desired, how much do you need to have in your investment portfolio? I will help you identify those issues. In addition, I will be offering ideas of things you might consider doing to help you redefine your retirement and help catch up to where you should be as you strive to achieve your dreams.

What is the Second Objective?

Please know the problem may not be yours alone. If you have many questions left unanswered, you must begin to ask if you have the right financial advisor and if your advisor has been asking the right questions. Later in a different chapter I will share with you how to find the right advisor. Our first meeting with a new prospect is a meeting that goes both ways. The prospect is trying to decide if we're the right advisor for them, and we are trying to decide if we are the right advisors for them and can truly help them. The way we can help this person is to ask a lot of questions.

Do you know what you want? In the next chapter I will be taking you through a question and answer session just as if you were sitting in my office. If you have taken the time already to identify some or all of the things you want, great! The next chapter will help us expand upon those answers.

CHAPTER 3

Signs that Your Retirement Plan is in Danger

Remember the year 2008? If not, you didn't have any money invested anywhere. The stock market fell 37% that year. Many people I met with coming from other financial institutions had lost as much as 50 to 60% of their portfolio in a single year.

Regardless of how much money you may have lost in 2008, there are eight indicators that you can focus on that would help you identify if you were taking too much risk in your portfolio and if your retirement plan was in danger.

Indicator 1:

You either looked at your accounts every day OR you wouldn't look at them at all.

Many could not believe that this was happening to them. If you looked at your account every day then you could be considered a sadistic person who loved pain. However, you couldn't help yourself. Your broker would constantly say one of two things: a) Just hang in there, it's going to come back, or b) You never invest for the short term in the market. Then they would go on into his or her memorized speech about how over any 20 year period of time the market is the best place to be.

If you were 25 years old, this **may** have been good advice. However, for someone within 10 years of retirement or God forbid already retired, this is a disastrous statement by any financial advisor.

This "advice" from brokers led many to stop looking at their accounts. When their monthly statements came in, they would either take a deep breath and peek, only to find that pit in their stomach again or they would refuse to open the statement and just pile them up in the corner. Their broker, was telling them to hold on. **This is a sign your retirement plan is in danger!**

Indicator 2:

You lost more than 15 to 20% of your investments value in 2008.

Later in Chapter 6, we will be talking about strategies to better protect your portfolio from a major market fall. We'll be discussing how you can be back in charge of just how risky your investments are instead of solely depending on your broker or financial planner. Don't get me wrong, this is not a book designed to beat up on financial professionals, after all I am one and most people can benefit from their input and advice. However, you should never put ALL of your faith in your advisor leaving your future totally in their hands without you having some say. Chapter 5 will help you learn how to take charge of your portfolio and manage the risk according to your risk tolerance, not the risk tolerance that a planner thinks is the right one for you.

When clients come into our office, I will many times ask them a simple question, "On a scale of 1 to 10, with 10 being your willingness to take risk on your investments and 1 being you hate risk of any kind, what number would you be?" Invariably, I would get a higher number. However, after asking some additional questions I would identify that the number was actually much lower than they first suggested. The only way to properly identify their true risk tolerance was with more in-depth questions.

The next problem is that the gap between what your advisor sees as the appropriate investments for your risk tolerance level and what you would see as the appropriate investments. This gap can often times be worlds apart.

I have on countless occasions had prospective clients come for their initial interview and identified them as a three on a risk level of 1 to 10 only to find that the financial advisor had them invested at a level of 7. Time after time, potentially new clients would come in having lost 30 to 50% of their portfolio only to have them tell me, "I told my advisor I didn't want that much risk." In fairness, sometimes they were right about that statement. Other times, they only became that conservative after losing so much money. Either way, I believe it is important to teach consumers how to monitor the level of risk they are in and what a properly diversified portfolio matching their risk levels looks like. It's time for all investors to be taught how they can once again be in control of these issues instead of solely depending on their financial advisor to pick what the right investments and level of risk is for them. After all, it is not the advisors money. It's your money, and they will almost always be willing to take more risk on your money than you may want to. **Losing 15 to 20% or more in your portfolio in 2008 is a sign your retirement plan is in danger.**

Indicator 3:

Your broker or financial advisor tells you to "just hang in there."

If you ever hear this advice from your broker or advisor, then you could be taking too much risk. This is not to say that a well-designed financial plan won't ever lose money. If that's the case, it's not a well-designed plan. Any properly designed "financial plan" will most likely have some elements that will lose value at some point. However, the key is how has your overall portfolio performed? If you have twenty different investments in your portfolio and investments number 2, 5 and 12 lose some value, but the other 17 areas increase in value thereby meaning your portfolio either broke even or gained, you have a well-designed portfolio.

I many times must admit that my more conservative investors will call if a similar occurrence like the one just stated happens. They don't like the fact that the three accounts mentioned above lost ANY value. I respond by telling them why this happened and what the outlook for the future is on those three accounts. If I believe they will do well in the future, I will communicate and educate them as to why they should hold onto those investments. Once I do this, they then can make an educated decision as to what they wish to do at that time. **But, it's their decision not mine.**

Other times, I will recommend they eliminate a position or make a change. But in all cases, patience and proper education are key. However, in no case do I say, "just hang in there." That is the advice you get from one of two advisors: a) the one who is lazy and thinks of themselves as so much smarter than you so you should just trust them, or b) the one who has no idea why the investment did what it did and has no good advice on what to do out of ignorance. **Either way, if you ever hear the words "JUST HANG IN THERE," it's a sign your retirement portfolio is in danger (and you may want to consider a change).**

Indicator 4:

Your broker or financial advisor fails to call you on a regular basis.

One of the most common complaints I hear from potential clients is that they never hear from their financial advisor or broker. You should be hearing from your advisor on a regular basis to discuss your account. The only time this should not be the case is if you, the client, request something different. The investment world is far too volatile in today's economy to live by the old "buy and hold" and call me once a year approach. I have some clients ask me to only call or visit with them semi-annually, even a few that say once per year (although these are the clients who carry low risk in what they have chosen to do). Markets move every day. Regardless of how often you speak or hear from your advisor, in today's economy a "buy and hold" approach can cost you dearly in your retirement. You need and should demand "active" management of your portfolio.

Does your broker call you more than quarterly? You would think this is wonderful to get that kind of service from them. However, this could be a sign of a dangerous amount of risk. It could be commission motivated and not in your best interest.

Therefore, calls from your advisor too often could mean more risk. If they seldom call you, it should be because you requested it. Also, watch out for an advisor who is too busy finding new clients or just doesn't care enough. That can be a sign your retirement plan could be in danger.

Indicator 5:

Your portfolio is tied mostly to Wall Street or "stocks, bonds, and mutual funds."

In Chapter 5 we will again look at this in more detail. However, check your statements and ask yourself if each investment you have represents only a stock, a bond, or a stock or bond mutual fund. **If the answer is yes, then you are taking a potentially dangerous amount of risk in your portfolio.** See Chapter 5 for more details.

Indicator 6:

You depend on your bond portfolio to protect you in hard times.

From 1981 to 1999, for a period of almost 20 years, the public was taught that bonds are the place to be when times get tough. Most of the public when asked would say that their advisor had told them that he will "watch" their money for them and when times are good increase stock holdings. Then when times get bad he would decrease the amount of stocks in the account and increase bond holdings for greater safety. There are three problems with this:

- This isn't 1981 through 1999. Times have changed.

- They never truly "watch" your money.

- You end up hearing "just hang in there" which wouldn't be the case if they truly were watching your money.

Why did it work from 1981 to 1999? Because bonds have an inverse relationship to interest rates, ask yourself this question, *when during your entire lifetime have interest rates ever been lower than they are today?* Answer: NEVER! For the past 30 years, interest rates have for the most part been falling. This means that bonds have done well and did actually provide a safe haven for money as the stock market became too risky. However, with rates at their lowest point in any living generations lifetime, what are the odds of rates continuing to go down versus going up over the next 3 to 5 years? The answer by every audience around the country I have spoken to is "there is an excellent chance interest rates will be going up not down." Since bonds do the opposite of interest rates, then this would mean very bad news for the future of bond values (especially bond mutual funds) in the years to come.

So, now where will your advisor move your assets (if they even do) to protect them from a falling market? Most advisors have no idea and still show no concern over learning about alternative strategies and investments to better protect you.

If your advisor is still suggesting that you use bonds within your portfolio as THE alternative to a falling market, this is a sign your retirement plan may be in danger.

Indicator 7:

You worry a lot about money.

Do you find yourself often thinking about your money or feeling fear about your ability to retire? If so, this could be a sign that your retirement plan is in danger. It also would stem from three possibilities.

- Your fear is due to being invested in more risky positions than you would like.

- You really don't understand what you even are invested in.

- You don't have a clear cut plan to achieve your financial objectives.

1. Your fear is due to being invested in more risky positions than you would like. We have already covered this earlier in this chapter. It's time for a change of advisors who will be able to give you more comfort in your portfolio allocations

2. You really don't understand what you are invested in. If this is the case, your advisor is not educating you nor calling you as often as they should. This should lead you to question, "Why am I paying them?"

3. You don't have a clear cut plan to achieve your financial objectives. This results when your advisor never presents a well-drawn up "plan" on how to help your reach your objectives. Instead, they are *selling* investments not presenting strategies and plans. There are no goals or targets determined. There are no hard targets along the way or dates to achieve certain objectives. There are no indications of points that must be reached along the way to help you know if you are on track to reach your ultimate goals instead of waiting to the end only to find out you have fallen short of your retirement goals. Now it is too late! Your approach designed by your planner is "Trust me to do what's right" and your left with nothing more than hoping you can reach your dreams. It's time to uncross your fingers and find another advisor.

If you are worrying often about money or your ability to be able to retire, your retirement plan is in danger.

Indicator 8:

You find you are short with people more than usual.

Do you find yourself short with others, on edge, more critical than usual? Family members are asking, "What's up with him or her?" This could stem from many reasons, not just your investments.

However, if most of life seems normal with the exception of your concern over retirement needs or money, then this could be a sign your retirement plan is in danger. Maybe it's time for a change.

Why Most Retirement Plans Will Fail and How to Make Sure Yours Isn't One of Them

Most advisors who are advising today have only been in the business since 1979 or thereafter and therein is the problem! While we all believe in experience as a critical factor in getting good advice, in the financial services world it can hurt you if your advisor hasn't continued to grow in their knowledge during those years. Let me explain.

Most of you reading this book will remember the inflationary times we came through during Jimmy Carter's era as President of the United States. As mentioned before, 1979 to 1981 were some of the worst periods of inflation in our nation's history. Inflation reached the level of 21.5% at its peak. At that rate, the cost of goods and services were doubling every 3.5 years. While peak inflation didn't last long enough to cause that to come true, we can't forget the days when banks were paying 16% interest on a certificate of deposit.

You probably are thinking if I could only get 16% on a bank CD today, I would dump the stock market and put all of my money into CD's. If you did, you would be losing money at the rate of 5% per year with inflation over 21%. So, it's not quite as good as you first may have thought when you look at it from that standpoint.

What does this have to do with the potential failure of many retirement plans? In Chapter 3 I talked about the relationship of interest rates to the value of bonds. Let's look a little closer at how most advisors have represented their clients over the last 30 years.

You may recall a visit like this one. You went in to see your advisor and they drew a pie chart like this.

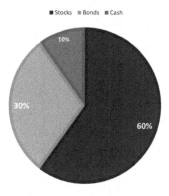

They said, "When the market is going well, we will increase your stock holdings and decrease your bonds and cash. However, if the market looks scary, I will call you and let you know that we need to reduce your stock holdings and increase your bonds and cash. This way we can make sure that you are always riding the positive swings in the market by overweighting stocks in the good times while overweighting bonds in the bad times to protect you when the market goes down."

Let me ask, how did that worked for you in 2008 when the market fell by 37%?

Most people have heard the famous line that all stock brokers are taught to say when they don't have an answer to you losing your money. We have referred earlier to the famous line, **"Just hang in there. The market will come back!"**

Isn't it easy to say that when it's not YOUR MONEY that's losing 37% of its value? What happened to the idea that your bonds would protect you? Why didn't your advisor call and recommend more bonds? Most likely they were too busy with their next prospect.

If they aren't moving your money as they promised, then they have you in a "Buy and Hold" Strategy. Why? Because they tell you what to buy and then you are supposed to just hold on to those investments forever. If that's the case, what good is it to have a financial advisor? When do you ever need a professional's advice again if all you are to do is sit on what you are first sold?

To me the greatest injustice is how brokers and financial planners seem to give the same advice to all age groups. They find stocks, bonds or mutual funds that they truly like and then sell those investments to all of their clients regardless of age or financial goals.

Is the buy and hold strategy the right strategy for every investor and under all financial circumstances? Or, is it simply the only advice brokers have known for the last 30 years? Unfortunately, I believe it is the latter.

Why then do so many brokers teach a buy and hold strategy for your retirement? I believe it's a) what they were taught to teach, or b) all they have known to do during their careers.

If that's all they know, how can they be expected to teach you anything different?

I must admit, that the buy and hold strategy worked well in the 80s and 90s. The reason for this is that we had the greatest period of prosperity and economic growth we have ever known as a nation. However, I don't believe it will work for at least another 6 years and maybe not for another 15 years.

Therefore if you are in or nearing retirement, understanding what I am sharing in this chapter could make or break your retirement years. It can be the difference between a great retirement and ending up depending on your children or falling into poverty. The buy and hold strategy hasn't worked as a strategy for the past 11 years. Here is why.

Bonds have an inverse relationship to interest rates. When interest rates fall (as they did from 1982 to 2014), bonds tend to go up in value. Therefore, when a broker showed you the pie chart with stocks, bonds, and cash, it was a good strategy. If stocks happened to fall while interest rates were falling, your bonds would increase in value and protect some of the losses you realized in your stocks. Also, we were in a 20 year bull market from 1981 to 1999. While some might argue the idea of a 20 year bull market, with little exception the stock market went from 1,000 to over 11,000 during that period of time. That's a 1000% return and one of the greatest bull markets we may ever see.

However, sometimes the longer the number of years the market climbs straight up, the longer the down swing that can follow. You may have heard it referred to as a bubble. That bubble began to burst in 2000 when the stock market fell over 9%. In 2001, it fell another 11%, and in 2002 it fell another 22%. Total the losses up without compounding them and that equates to over a 42% loss. Then in 2008, the market fell 37% in one year. However, what many people missed was that it fell another 22% in the first ten weeks of 2009 for a total uncompounded loss of almost 50%. For retirees, this was financial suicide. What did their brokers say? "Just hang in there!" Hanging in there makes sense for those who have 10 years or more until they retire. For those in retirement or close to it, it can destroy them.

I believe for at least the next 3 to 6 years we will continue to see the same type of market that we did from 2000 to 2016. I base this on two major premises.

- I believe the current state of our economy currently offers no hope in the near future of a possible bull market. Consider that in the first three months after Congress raised the debt ceiling that they have spent 500 billion more than we as a nation take in. Our total debt as of April 2016 exceeds 19.2 Trillion dollars. We are witnessing economic instability in Europe with Greece on the verge of collapse and closely followed by Italy, Portugal, Spain, and Ireland. While the dollar at the time of this writing was strong against other currencies, there is talk of no longer using the dollar as the international currency. Does this sound like the beginning of a bull market?

- We have been in four sideways markets in history (I will teach you more on a sideways market later in this chapter). The shortest one was 13 years and the longest one was 27 years. We were in a sideways market until 2013 and will likely be again in upcoming years.

If your advisor doesn't see this or understand the change and continues to advise you in the same way he or she has over the last 16 years, it could destroy your retirement! Here's why. As I stated earlier, interest rates are now at a level so low, no one reading this book has ever witnessed in their lifetime. Bank savings accounts are paying one quarter of one percent. CD's are paying less than 1% interest in most cases. Mortgage rates are in the 3% to 4% range.

One reason to expect inflation is the printing of money by the Federal Reserve. For a period of 48 years, from 1960 through 2008, the U.S. printed on average 6.6% new money each year.

For each $100 of U.S. currency floating in the world, they would print $6.60 of new money while taking some out of circulation as old and worn out. In just the first seven months of 2009, the government printed 109% of the U.S. money. A definite increase in printing. In 2014 according to www.moneyfactory.gov, the Treasury printed 6,006,400,000 new notes ranging from $1 to $100 bills… phew!

I believe it is worth repeating that if the Federal Reserve/Treasury were to print enough new money (which I doubt, but to make a point) and as a result double the amount of U.S. money in the world, each dollar would now only be worth .50 cents. To put that into perspective, imagine an ink pen in your home that possibly cost you $1. In order for the manufacturer to provide the same pen to you that you bought for $1, he must now charge $2 to get the same $1 as before. Why? Each dollar is now only worth 50 cents due to the fact that there is now double the U.S. currency in circulation worldwide.

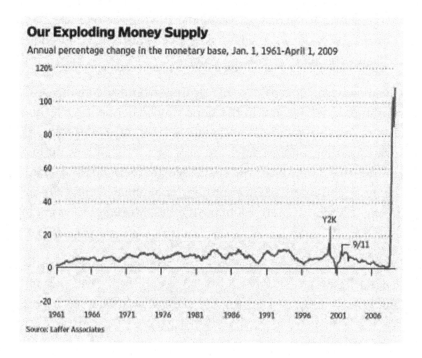

Our Exploding Money Supply
Annual percentage change in the monetary base, Jan. 1, 1961-April 1, 2009

Source: Laffer Associates

WHY MOST RETIREMENT PLANS WILL FAIL

Now, what do you think that would do to a retiree trying to make ends meet on a limited supply of assets if their income was cut in half by inflation?

Let's get back to the buy and hold strategy. Imagine now that your stock investments are falling (which they will again) and interest rates are climbing. What does that mean for your bond portfolio that your advisor believes in so strongly? If your bond holdings are in specific bonds with maturity dates, it means bad news if you were to ever need to sell them as they will all be losing value right along with the stock market. If your bonds holdings are all in mutual funds, it means extremely bad news as there is no set date of maturity in which you get your principal back. They have so many bond holdings within a mutual fund that the share price is adjusted as people sell out of the funds and there is no opportunity to hold each bond in the fund until they mature.

Please don't misunderstand me. Bonds are great investments when held at the right time for the right reasons and in the right economic environment. I don't think long term bonds or bond mutual funds would be the right investment for many people with the threat of rising interest rates and inflation.

You might be thinking, "Well why not hold just short term bonds and then I don't have to worry about losing money due to rising interest rates." Your assumption would be correct, however, now all you have to do is worry about earning a mere 1 to 2% (due to the bonds being a very short duration) while inflation is taking off. That still means you're in a losing position.

What does this mean to the retiree? If your broker is giving you the same advice he was giving you 10 and 20 years ago, you need a new broker who is current and investing his own time and money into strategies that will help you weather the economic storm we find ourselves in.

Which way will the market go and what does that mean to your retirement?

The best I can tell, there are only three things the stock market can do.

The market can go up.

The market can go down.

The market can go sideways.

I do not believe the stock market will go steadily up in the next decade nor do I believe it will go steadily down. I believe we are in a sideways market. Does this mean the market goes sideways over the next 10 years as in a straight line like this?

Does it stay at its current value and never move for 10 years? Not at all. Rather it looks something like this:

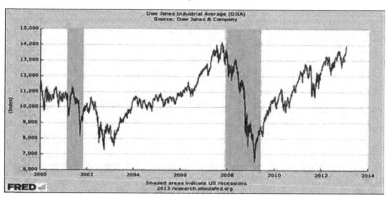

It goes up and down, but 10 years from now it will still be around the same value it is today. For a retiree this is trouble. If you had $100,000 in an account that lost 50% of its value, you would now have $50,000. However, to get back to $100,000 you don't need a 50% return. You need a 100% return. As a retiree, every time you lose money it takes a bigger percentage return to gain back what you have lost.

It is important to understand that before retirement we are in the "accumulation" stage of life. As we begin to save and accumulate money in our 20s and 30s, it really doesn't matter if the market is going up or down because we are *dollar cost averaging* (a system whereby you add a steady stream of money into your market investments each month regardless if the market is going up or down). Many times this is best represented by payroll deduction plans depositing into your account on a monthly basis. It can also be done through your bank on an automatic deduction from your bank account. This can still be profitable. Look at the example below.

Date	Amount Invested	Price per Share	Shares Purchased
January	$416.66	$33.21	12.55
February	$416.66	$35.70	11.67
March	$416.66	$34.83	11.96
April	$416.66	$32.10	12.98
May	$416.66	$33.71	12.36
June	$416.66	$35.08	11.88
July	$416.66	$29.04	14.35
August	$416.66	$28.17	14.79
September	$416.66	$27.92	14.92
October	$416.66	$25.83	16.13
November	$416.66	$26.42	15.77
December	$416.66	$28.18	14.79
Total shares	$4999.92	$30.46 avg.	164.15

You can see that while the market is losing money, we are buying cheaper shares. Then as the market comes back, all of the shares we bought on sale now grow to a larger value and our portfolio as a whole benefits from this approach.

However once we retire, we no longer live in the "accumulation" stage of life. We now transfer into the "distribution" stage of life (the stage where we are no longer working and putting savings into an investment portfolio). This is something totally different. Yet, how many brokers give their clients the same advice in the distribution stage (their retirement years) as they do while they are younger and accumulating money during the accumulation stage?

When in the distribution stage of life, we are now depending on what we have saved to help provide our income needs. The main goal in the distribution stage/retirement years now becomes DON'T LOSE MONEY!

Losing money in the first 5 years of retirement could destroy your financial security!

Let's look at the Accumulation chart on page 41 and 42.

The chart is broken into two main columns. The only difference is the order of returns. The returns shown are purely hypothetical and not reflecting any actual returns of the market in the past.

The rates of return in the columns on the right are identical to the columns on the left. The only difference is I flipped the interest rates. Look at years 1 through 5 of each side. Now look at years 26 through 30 on each side. I simply reversed the order that rates of return earned based on the market over a 30 year period. The rates on the top of one side are now on the bottom of the other side of the chart.

The important fact is that the columns on the right now suffer some losses in the first 5 years due to negative markets, while the columns on the left during the first 5 years are all positive returns.

You will notice that while accumulating assets, it has no impact whatsoever if and when you lose money in the market. You would end up with the same amount of money regardless of when the negative years occurred.

Accumulation
The "Upside" of the Mountain

Illustrated Index				
Year	Age	Beginning Amount	Yearly Return	End of Year Value
1	65	$ 500,000	8%	$ 540,000
2	66	$ 540,000	-16%	$ 453,600
3	67	$ 453,600	-12%	$ 399,168
4	68	$ 399,168	27%	$ 506,943
5	69	$ 506,943	23%	$ 623,540
6	70	$ 623,540	-15%	$ 530,009
7	71	$ 530,009	22%	$ 646,611
8	72	$ 646,611	18%	$ 763,001
9	73	$ 763,001	-12%	$ 871,441
10	74	$ 871,441	20%	$ 805,729
11	75	$ 805,729	14%	$ 918,532
12	76	$ 918,532	-6%	$ 863,420
13	77	$ 863,420	18%	$ 1,018,832
14	78	$ 1,018,832	12%	$ 1,141,095
15	79	$ 1,141,095	-6%	$ 1,072,630
16	80	$ 1,072,630	23%	$ 1,319,335
17	81	$ 1,319,335	31%	$ 1,728,328
18	82	$ 1,728,328	-5%	$ 1,641,912
19	83	$ 1,641,912	11%	$ 1,822,522
20	84	$ 1,822,522	3%	$ 1,877,198
21	85	$ 1,877,198	23%	$ 2,308,953
22	86	$ 2,308,953	18%	$ 2,724,565
23	87	$ 2,724,565	-6%	$ 2,561,091
24	88	$ 2,561,091	18%	$ 3,022,087
25	89	$ 3,022,087	5%	$ 2,870,983
26	90	$ 2,870,983	19%	$ 3,416,470
27	91	$ 3,416,470	5%	$ 3,587,293
28	92	$ 3,587,293	11%	$ 3,981,896
29	93	$ 3,981,896	6%	$ 4,220,809
30	94	$ 4,220,809	18%	$ 4,980,555

Accumulation
The "Downside" of the Mountain

Illustrated Index Reversed				
Year	Age	Beginning Amount	Yearly Return	End of Year Value
1	65	$ 500,000	18%	$ 590,000
2	66	$ 590,000	6%	$ 625,400
3	67	$ 625,194	11%	$ 694,194
4	68	$ 694,194	5%	$ 728,904
5	69	$ 728,904	19%	$ 867,395
6	70	$ 867,395	-5%	$ 824,026
7	71	$ 824,026	18%	$ 972,350
8	72	$ 972,350	-6%	$ 914,009
9	73	$ 914,009	18%	$ 1,078,531
10	74	$ 1,078,531	23%	$ 1,326,593
11	75	$ 1,326,593	3%	$ 1,366,391
12	76	$ 1,366,391	11%	$ 1,516,694
13	77	$ 1,516,694	-5%	$ 1,440,859
14	78	$ 1,440,859	31%	$ 1,887,525
15	79	$ 1,887,525	23%	$ 2,321,656
16	80	$ 2,321,656	-6%	$ 2,182,357
17	81	$ 2,182,357	12%	$ 2,444,240
18	82	$ 2,444,240	18%	$ 2,884,203
19	83	$ 2,884,203	-6%	$ 2,711,151
20	84	$ 2,711,151	14%	$ 3,090,712
21	85	$ 3,090,712	20%	$ 3,708,854
22	86	$ 3,708,854	-12%	$ 3,263,792
23	87	$ 3,263,792	18%	$ 3,851,274
24	88	$ 3,851,274	22%	$ 4,698,554
25	89	$ 4,698,554	-15%	$ 3,993,771
26	90	$ 3,993,771	23%	$ 4,912,339
27	91	$ 4,912,339	27%	$ 6,238,670
28	92	$ 6,238,670	-12%	$ 5,490,030
29	93	$ 5,490,030	-16%	$ 4,611,625
30	94	$ 4,611,625	8%	$ 4,980,555

The important part of this is that when ACCUMULAT
ASSETS in your younger years you can afford the risk o
market better.

**LOSING MONEY WHILE IN RETIREMENT CAN DESTROY
YOUR ECONOMIC FUTURE.**

Now look at the next chart. The "Distribution" chart on pages 44
and 45.

You will notice virtually the same chart and rates of return as on
the accumulation chart. The only difference is that you now may
need to depend on your assets for income in retirement. I have
used an example of this person pulling out $35,000 per year of
income or 7% of his portfolio value.

As you can see in the "yearly returns" column where there were
no losses in the first 5 years, there is no negative impact. The
investor's assets did the job and provided for him or her entire
retirement. Now look at the "yearly returns" column on the next
graph, where the market loses in two of the first 5 years. This
person is broke at the age of 82.

The only difference was losing money in the first 5 years while
taking a distribution.

The point of this is that when DISTRIBUTING ASSETS in your
retirement years you may not be able to afford the risk of a buy
and hold strategy in the stock market.

In the next chapter, I will begin to share how you can be in total
control of how your money is invested and identify a way to better
communicate with your financial professional as to what you
would like your portfolio to look like.

Distribution/Withdrawls
The "Upside" of the Mountain

		Illustrated Index			
Year	Age	Beginning Amount	Yearly Return	Annual Withdrawal	End of Year Value
1	65	$ 500,000	18%	$35,000	$ 555,250
2	66	$ 555,250	6%	$36,050	$ 552,250
3	67	$ 552,250	11%	$37,132	$ 575,866
4	68	$ 575,866	5%	$38,245	$ 566,414
5	69	$ 566,414	19%	$39,393	$ 634,640
6	70	$ 634,640	–5%	$40,575	$ 562,333
7	71	$ 562,333	18%	$41,792	$ 621,761
8	72	$ 621,761	–6%	$43,048	$ 541,410
9	73	$ 541,410	18%	$44,337	$ 594,527
10	74	$ 594,527	23%	$45,667	$ 685,601
11	75	$ 685,601	3%	$47,037	$ 659,132
12	76	$ 659,132	11%	$48,448	$ 683,188
13	77	$ 683,188	–5%	$49,902	$ 599,127
14	78	$ 599,127	31%	$51,399	$ 733,458
15	79	$ 733,458	23%	$52,941	$ 849,213
16	80	$ 849,213	–6%	$54,529	$ 743,731
17	81	$ 743,731	12%	$56,165	$ 776,814
18	82	$ 776,814	18%	$57,850	$ 858,791
19	83	$ 858,791	–6%	$59,585	$ 747,678
20	84	$ 747,678	14%	$61,373	$ 790,980
21	85	$ 790,980	20%	$63,214	$ 885,963
22	86	$ 885,963	–12%	$66,110	$ 714,537
23	87	$ 714,537	18%	$67,064	$ 776,090
24	88	$ 776,090	22%	$69,076	$ 877,754
25	89	$ 877,754	–15%	$71,148	$ 674,943
26	90	$ 674,943	23%	$73,282	$ 756,898
27	91	$ 756,898	27%	$75,481	$ 885,780
28	92	$ 885,780	–12%	$77,745	$ 701,741
29	93	$ 701,741	–16%	$80,077	$ 509,385
30	94	$ 509,385	8%	$82,480	$ 467,656

Distribution/Withdrawls
The "Downside" of the Mountain

		Illustrated Index Reversed			
Year	Age	Beginning Amount	Yearly Return	Annual Withdrawal	End of Year Value
1	65	$ 500,000	8%	$35,000	$ 505,000
2	66	$ 505,000	–16%	$36,050	$ 388,150
3	67	$ 388,150	–12%	$37,132	$ 304,441
4	68	$ 304,441	27%	$38,245	$ 348,394
5	69	$ 348,394	23%	$39,393	$ 389,132
6	70	$ 389,132	–15%	$40,575	$ 290,187
7	71	$ 290,187	22%	$41,792	$ 312,237
8	72	$ 312,237	18%	$43,048	$ 325,394
9	73	$ 325,394	–12%	$44,337	$ 242,010
10	74	$ 242,010	20%	$45,667	$ 244,745
11	75	$ 244,745	14%	$47,037	$ 231,972
12	76	$ 231,972	–6%	$48,448	$ 169,605
13	77	$ 169,605	18%	$49,902	$ 150,233
14	78	$ 150,233	12%	$51,399	$ 116,862
15	79	$ 116,862	–6%	$52,941	$ 56,909
16	80	$ 56,909	23%	$54,529	$ 15,470
17	81	$ 15,470	31%	$56,165	$ (35,899)
18	82	$ (35,899)	–5%	$57,850	$ (91,954)
19	83	$ (91,954)	11%	$59,585	$ (161,654)
20	84	$ (161,654)	34%	$61,373	$ (227,877)
21	85	$ (227,877)	23%	$63,214	$ (343,502)
22	86	$ (343,502)	18%	$66,110	$ (470,443)
23	87	$ (470,443)	–6%	$67,064	$ (509,280)
24	88	$ (509,280)	18%	$69,076	$ (670,026)
25	89	$ (670,026)	–5%	$71,148	$ (707,672)
26	90	$ (707,672)	19%	$73,282	$ (915,412)
27	91	$ (915,412)	5%	$75,481	$ (1,036,663)
28	92	$ (1,036,663)	11%	$77,745	$ (1,228,442)
29	93	$ (1,228,442)	6%	$80,077	$ (1,382,225)
30	94	$ (1,382,225)	18%	$82,480	$(1,714,506)

Questions That Will Change Your Life!

In order to do this properly, I will pretend that we are actually sitting in front of each other and I'll be asking you questions. These would be the same questions I would ask someone new to our office. I will be giving you some hints and tips along the way. It's my hope that the questions will help you develop clarity surrounding your retirement goals and dreams. The key to your retirement lays not in stocks, bonds and mutual funds. It does not lay in how good you are at picking the right investment. The key to your financial future lies solely and totally in the strategies can come from completing the type of questions in this form.

Here we go then.

What specifically brought you into visit with us today?

Your answer to this question should be based upon what concerns you today. In other words, as you look at your financial portfolio and your advisors (financial planner, CPA, tax practitioner, or attorney), what is it that concerns you today? What is it that caused you to seek out help from another person like myself? Take a moment before you read on and fill in the blank space below and answer that question.

_____

_____

_____

_____

_____

The things that concern me the most are:

_____

_____

_____

_____

_____

Specifically, how does it make you feel knowing that these concerns and problems are present?

_____

_____

_____

_____

_____

If we could resolve these problems for you, how would that change your outlook on your retirement?

_____

_____

_____

_____

_____

Describe the ideal retirement for you and your spouse. Where will you live?

_____

_____

Will you have one home or two?

_____

_____

Are there any hobbies that you or your spouse enjoy that you just haven't gotten around to because of time demands? If so, what are they?

_____

_____

_____

_____

_____

Would you like to travel? If there were three locations that you definitely want to go to during your retirement, where would they be?

_____

_____

_____

_____

_____

Do you have any other goals or dreams for your retirement that you would like to list?

_____

_____

_____

_____

_____

Do you own a home?   ☐ Yes   ☐ No

If yes, what is the current market value of your home?

$ _____

What is the mortgage balance on that home?

$ _____

Equity on home? (value minus mortgage)

$ _____

Do you own any other real estate?   ☐ Yes ☐ No

If yes, what is the combined current market value of all other real estate owned?

$ _____

What is its mortgage balance, if any?

$ _____

What is your equity? (value minus mortgage)

$ _____

What is your cost basis for all other real estate?

$ _____

Do you have a pension?   ☐ Yes ☐ No

If yes, what is the monthly amount you receive/will receive each month?

Yours $ _____

Spouses $ _____

Does it reduce at either spouse's death?   ☐ Yes
☐ No If yes, to what amount?

Yours $ _____

Spouses $ _____

What is your date of birth?

Yours _____

Spouses _____

What is your current or projected Social Security income per month?

Yours $_____ (current)

         $_____ (projected at age 66/67)

Spouses $_____ (current)

         $_____ (projected at age 66/67)

Do you have any other sources of monthly or annual income?

       ☐ Yes   ☐ No

If yes, list your other sources of income

Source: _____

$_____ per month/year

Source: _____

$_____ per month/year

Source: _____

$_____ per month/year

Are you currently retired?   ☐ Yes   ☐ No

If no, how many years until you plan to do so?

How many retirement years would you like to plan for? (I realize no one knows the date they may die but at least list how long you want to make sure you are covered with income and assets)

_____

Number of years for retirement to last? _____

What income do you feel you would need to be able to retire in TODAY'S DOLLARS? (please be realistic)

Income needed per year (after tax) $ _____

Did you claim any interest income last year?   ☐ Yes ☐ No

If yes, how much? (found on line 8A of your tax return)

Interest income $ _____

Did you claim any "ordinary dividends" on your tax return for last year?   ☐ Yes ☐ No

If yes, how much? (found on line 9A of your tax return)

Ordinary Dividends: $ _____

What was the Social Security income listed on your tax return last year, if any? (found on line 20A of your tax return)

Social Security income last year? $ _____

Did you claim any of your Social Security payments as taxable income this past year? (found on line 20B of your tax return)

Social Security income claimed last year: $_____

How much life insurance do you carry? (If you are still working, do not claim insurance that you will lose once retired. Only count insurance that can follow you into retirement)

Total death benefit amount

Yours $ _____

Spouses $ _____

Cost of all insurance policies per year

Yours $ _____

Spouses $ _____

Current cash value of all policies, if any

Yours $ _____

Spouses $ _____

Please note that you should work with your advisor to identify the need, or lack thereof, for life insurance in your retirement years. There are many issues to consider other than paying for final expenses. You may need to cover some estate tax issues. You could lose a pension on the death of the first spouse, as well as some Social Security income and need to replace it. You may have charitable gifts that you would like to make. You may want some assets in trust for the benefit of your children or a special needs child. Make sure you consult a professional life insurance agent or your financial advisor to discuss these important issues.

If you are married this next question needs to be answered by both husband and wife. Answer independently of how the other person would respond. Don't worry about what your spouse's answer might be. Be honest with your own.

On a scale of 1 to 10, with 10 being your willingness to take risk on your investments and 1 indicating you don't like risk of any kind, circle the number you would be?

You   1   2   3   4   5   6   7   8   9   10

Spouse   1   2   3   4   5   6   7   8   9   10

While I love my children, I am only worried about providing for my (and spouse's) retirement. ☐ Yes ☐ No

While supporting my retirement is my number one concern, it would be important to me to leave a financial legacy to my children as well. ☐ Yes ☐ No

Do you have a will? ☐ Yes   ☐ No
When was the last year it was updated? _____

Do you have a trust?   ☐ Yes ☐ No
When was the last year it was updated? _____

Do you plan, or would you like to leave any, charitable gifts (if you could do so without hurting your retirement or family)? These could be organizations that mean something to you such as your church, missions, American Cancer Society, or other similar organization.   ☐ Yes ☐ No

List the names of organizations that might be important to you.

1. _____

2. _____

3. _____

4. _____

5. _____

6. _____

7. _____

8. _____

If I had the privilege of serving you as a client and 3 years from now we were sitting together, what would need to have happened for you to be satisfied and happy with our professional relationship together? *The R-Factor Question®

_____

_____

_____

_____

_____

_____

_____

_____

_____

_____

_____

_____

_____

_____

_____

Your Current Investments:

Account #1

First name ONLY on account

_____

This investment is with (i.e.: Merrill Lynch, Morgan Stanley, American Funds, Scottrade, etc.)

_____

The title on the account is (circle one)

JTWROS   Single Name Trust   IRA Roth

IRA   Co. Retirement Plan

Total value of all stocks, bonds, mutual funds, and variable annuities ONLY within the account

$ _____

Total value of all "alternative investments" (REITS (real estate investment trusts), second homes or property you own, gold, silver, equipment leasing programs) within the account

$ _____

Total value of all guaranteed investments (bank accounts, fixed annuities, fixed or equity index annuities, federally backed bonds) within the account

$ _____

Account #2 (if needed)

First name ONLY on account

This investment is with (i.e.: Merrill Lynch, Morgan Stanley, American Funds, Scottrade, etc.)

The title on the account is (circle one)

JTWROS   Single Name Trust   IRA Roth

IRA   Co. Retirement Plan

Total value of all stocks, bonds, mutual funds, and variable annuities ONLY within the account

$ _____

Total value of all "alternative investments" (REITS (real estate investment trusts), second homes or property you own, gold, silver, equipment leasing programs) within the account

$ _____

Total value of all guaranteed investments (bank accounts, fixed annuities, fixed or equity index annuities, federally backed bonds) within the account

$ _____

Account #3 (if needed)

First name ONLY on account

_____

This investment is with (i.e.: Merrill Lynch, Morgan Stanley, American Funds, Scottrade, etc.)

_____

The title on the account is (circle one)

JTWROS   Single Name Trust   IRA Roth

IRA   Co. Retirement Plan

Total value of all stocks, bonds, mutual funds, and variable annuities ONLY within the account

$ _____

Total value of all "alternative investments" (REITS (real estate investment trusts), second homes or property you own, gold, silver, equipment leasing programs) within the account

$ _____

Total value of all guaranteed investments (bank accounts, fixed annuities, fixed or equity index annuities, federally backed bonds) within the account

$ _____

Account #4 (if needed)

First name ONLY on account

_____

This investment is with (i.e.: Merrill Lynch, Morgan Stanley, American Funds, Scottrade, etc.)

_____

The title on the account is (circle one)

JTWROS   Single Name Trust   IRA Roth

IRA   Co. Retirement Plan

Total value of all stocks, bonds, mutual funds, and variable annuities ONLY within the account

$ _____

Total value of all "alternative investments" (REITS (real estate investment trusts), second homes or property you own, gold, silver, equipment leasing programs) within the account

$ _____

Total value of all guaranteed investments (bank accounts, fixed annuities, fixed or equity index annuities, federally backed bonds) within the account

$ _____

Account #5 (if needed)

First name ONLY on account

_____

This investment is with (i.e.: Merrill Lynch, Morgan Stanley, American Funds, Scottrade, etc.)

_____

The title on the account is (circle one)

JTWROS   Single Name Trust   IRA Roth

IRA   Co. Retirement Plan

Total value of all stocks, bonds, mutual funds, and variable annuities ONLY within the account

$ _____

Total value of all "alternative investments" (REITS (real estate investment trusts), second homes or property you own, gold, silver, equipment leasing programs) within the account

$ _____

Total value of all guaranteed investments (bank accounts, fixed annuities, fixed or equity index annuities, federally backed bonds) within the account

$ _____

Account #6 (if needed)

First name ONLY on account

_____

This investment is with (i.e.: Merrill Lynch, Morgan Stanley, American Funds, Scottrade, etc.)

_____

The title on the account is (circle one)

JTWROS   Single Name Trust   IRA Roth

IRA   Co. Retirement Plan

Total value of all stocks, bonds, mutual funds, and variable annuities ONLY within the account

$ _____

Total value of all "alternative investments" (REITS (real estate investment trusts), second homes or property you own, gold, silver, equipment leasing programs) within the account

$ _____

Total value of all guaranteed investments (bank accounts, fixed annuities, fixed or equity index annuities, federally backed bonds) within the account

$ _____

Has your advisor asked you these questions before? If so that's a great start.

Unfortunately I find that many advisors never really dive this deep into your financial life. Yet, after some brief questions, he/she can begin to recommend investments to you. In reality, they are investment salespeople. They can sometimes be likened to a car salesman (no offense to car salesman intended). A car salesperson may begin by asking what you are looking for. What kind of payments (risk) you are willing to take. What you wanted to spend on a car (or how much you want to invest) and then boom! Have I got the right car... oops... investment for you!

Your retirement is far too important to leave this to a salesman who may or may not be with the firm in 2 years, or who doesn't care enough to take the time to dig and make sure they create not just some investment ideas, but as you will learn and most importantly, help you identify or create for you strategies that can help meet your goals and dreams.

I hope this does not represent your advisor. If you feel you have a good advisor, take the answers to these questions to him/her and have another meeting to review and make sure your investments and strategies match your goals.

Finally, if you would like help in formulating a Red, Blue, Green analysis for you to take to your advisor, you can contact my office and we will send it along for your advisors review.

Here's to your future, a future that results in reaching your dreams and goals.

CHAPTER 6

Red, Blue, Green Putting You in Control

Jack Nicklaus is undisputedly one of the greatest golfers of all time. There is a current golfer who seems to be challenging Jack for this title and of course that would be Tiger Woods. Though Tiger has had his struggles of late with his image, no one can deny his greatness on the golf course. Time will tell if he can come back and return to his once level of superiority.

Let me ask you a question. What's more important, Tiger Woods or his golf clubs? I bet I could run out to Kmart and buy a set of the most inexpensive golf clubs and give them to Tiger Woods and give or take two or three strokes, he could possibly golf close to as well as he would with his own clubs. You see the magic to Tiger Woods and Jack Nicklaus is not their clubs. It's their swing! On countless occasions I've had the ability to golf with friends and associates only to find that they spent $300 to $400 maybe even $500 on a brand new driver because it promised that they could hit it further. And interestingly, their score never seems to change. They still stayed in the same range of scores they usually fell within. Why? It's not about the clubs. It's about their swing.

When looking at your financial investments, those are really the clubs in your investment portfolio. If you're looking to get a great return on a long-term investment, you want to hit the ball far down the course and get as much distance as you can. In golf, this would be your driver. Drivers can hit the ball the farthest, but can also cause the ball to go off target the most. If you wanted just a little chip shot up onto the green, you might pull out your sand wedge or your pitching wedge. Why? You usually are far more accurate with the shorter clubs. This would mean less distance, but far less risk of sending the ball off in the wrong direction.

Golf is a game of strategy and skill. If you don't use the right clubs for the right distance, you increase your risk of a poor score/result.

In building a portfolio for your retirement years, it's the same thing. The only difference is instead of clubs, you choose your investments. For a long drive, you would go to a higher risk stock or mutual fund that is more risky but could possibly provide long-term growth. A bond might represent, at times, a little less risk, but would not take your ball (growth) as far. However, just like golf, you need more than clubs; you need the right strategy (the right swing).

When taking lessons one time the golf pro asked me what iron I felt the most comfortable using. I told him my pitching wedge, which I usually hit about 110 yards. He then recommended that when coming down the fairway on a par five, if after my first shot I had 250 yards to go, instead of going for the green on my second shot (which at that distance I'd have little hope of achieving) to go for a 140 yard shot instead. This would call for my 7 or 8 iron, which I would be far more accurate with than a 3 wood, and my goal would be to lay up my second shot 110 yards from the green. This then would leave me at the perfect distance for the club I am most confident in (my pitching wedge). By using the wedge on my third shot, I'd have a much better chance of getting the ball closer to the pin and thereby have a better chance for a birdie on my fourth shot. That is a "strategy" to get a better score in golf. In the same way strategy is a major part of the game of investing.

In investing, if you don't have a strategy of your own, then you end up turning to a professional, as you should, for help in creating the right "customized strategy" for you. An investment advisor can be a coach for your investment strategy just as a golf pro is for a golfing strategy.

Do you just go out and start buying investments (swinging your investment clubs) or would it be smart to consider getting lessons along the way? Trying to secure your retirement without a strategy and without the right coach is like trying to lower your score by just continuing to swing away with any club in your bag. Remember practice DOESN'T make perfect; perfect practice helps you get closer to your goals.

Fortunately or unfortunately, depending on how you look at it, there are many financial coaches available to choose from. But not all financial coaches are the right ones for you. In the last chapter, I will address how you can find the right investment coach for your portfolio. For now though, let's talk about how financial advisors and brokers can let you down.

So now you realize you need a strategy and you need a financial coach. Your goal is to find a financial coach who will help you design a plan for your ideal retirement. However, you may not be sure how to get there or what investments (clubs) you will need. Most importantly, you need to develop the proper swing (be educated) so YOU can better judge the investments (clubs) you will need at each step of the plan and depending on the market conditions (weather). Your number one goal is to reach your goals with THE LEAST AMOUNT OF RISK POSSIBLE (you want to lower your score). You want a safer approach to your goals and the right strategies to do so. You want to **secure** your retirement.

What do many advisors do? They tell you about this really awesome stock or mutual fund that can hit the ball 350 yards, and, of course, they say with very little risk (just like on the TV commercials for that new driver). In investing terms they don't talk about your strategy or needs for your retirement goals. As a matter of fact, they don't even talk about setting goals or objectives, rather they tell you about the latest and greatest stock or investment that will help you get a 12% to 15% return (hit the ball farther down the fairway) instead of a 10% return (you can get an extra 20 yards) with this new investment (club).

Many advisors believe that it's all about the rate of return. They believe the advisor who gets you the best return (the one who can teach you to hit the ball the farthest) is the one that wins. But what about my overall strategy, you say? If they didn't ask you about your goals and then help you develop strategies to attain them, they really are nothing more than a salesman who makes a commission on what you buy. They figure if they can sell you an investment that has a better rate of return than the one you have now, you're going to jump ship, and you're going to buy their investment. Ladies and gentlemen, please don't fall prey to advisors/ salesman trying to sell you a fancier investment/ golf club.

First and foremost, you must identify what you want. Once we have a clear picture of what you want, we now have the swing down for the retirement you desire. The only remaining factor then is to develop a strategy that when applied with your swing will help you reach your retirement goals. Once the goals and strategies are laid out, we can then make sure we are choosing the right investment and more accurately predict where we are going to end up. But you must have the swing/strategy not to just pick clubs based on someone else's opinion of what those investments may or may not achieve regardless of your plans,

Unfortunately, helping you identify your goals and strategies is a custom thing for each individual reading this book. As much as I would like to help each of you with your individual strategies, it is impossible to do. The public today is bombarded with so called professional advisors on the radio and in print who lead you to believe their advice is the right advice. *The right advice can only be determined on a one-on-one basis*, not over the radio. What might be the right thing to do for a 35 year old client can be the worst thing a retiree can do. Yet there they are giving advice to everyone listening to the radio or reading their magazines as if it doesn't matter what your goals and strategies are; their advice is always right. **WRONG!**

For now, I would like to teach you how to never fall prey again to the wrong advisor and end up with more risk than you would intend to take or desire. This is a system I have used that has more safely guided our clients through the financial storms of the decade from 2000 through 2020. The system is called "Red, Blue, Green."

For the rest of this book, I will refer to Red, Blue and Green as RBG. RBG is a system that will help you know how much risk you are taking and put you back in control of that risk instead of what your advisor thinks is the right amount of risk.

Earlier, I spoke of clients coming into our offices stating they told their advisor they didn't want as much risk as they previously had. Yet they carried higher degrees of risk. Why? Because the advisors idea of risk and he clients idea of risk can be worlds apart.

Let's see how the colors can help you determine your risk.

Red Money

Red money investments are defined as the most popular investments that are tied to Wall Street. This would mean stocks, bonds and mutual funds for most of America. While there can be other investments that would qualify for this, they are seldom seen or used by most advisors. I base this on my experience in looking at countless statements from potentially new clients in our offices. If you did have Wall Street investments that are not in these three general categories, you probably wouldn't be reading this book.

Blue Money

Blue money represents investments that are often referred to as "Alternative Investments". These are many times things like Real Estate Trusts (REITS), equipment leasing programs, precious metals, like gold and silver, High Grade Rare Coins, and collectibles.

Over the last decade of 2000-2009, these investments have been a critical part of our client's investment portfolios. Yet, we seldom see many of these (if any) in potential client's accounts when they visit us. The key to this part of RBG is it can help create a portion of the portfolio that has historically created good income or a low correlation to the stock market.

Green Money

Green Money quite simply is accounts that come with a guarantee of some sort. They are either backed by the FDIC, the Legal Reserve System which is supported by the insurance industry, or insurance companies themselves. To put it simply, these are investments in your portfolio that have guarantees to not lose your principal (and sometimes even your earnings).

Why Red, Blue, Green?

Not everyone learns best through visual illustrations, some people learn better through hearing as an example. However, I have never met anyone yet, that when using RBG to show them the current diversification and risk in their portfolio, didn't find it a major benefit in helping them make better investment decisions.

Let's look at what a RBG chart would look like for a typical person or couple coming into our office.

As you can see, this graph is mostly made up of Wall Street investments (Red). Is it any wonder why when 2008 came along this sample client lost up to 50% or more of their investments? In 2008, the stock market lost 37%. I had some new potential clients who had lost 25 to 30% with their broker and others who lost up to 80% of their portfolio! Either way, if you are within 5 years of retirement or older, that is catastrophic!

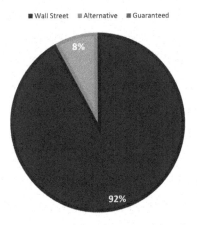

Once a prospective client sees the amount of red in their chart, they almost instantly say, "I didn't want that much risk!" Now, they can be in control of the risk they carry. How? Because they can see a picture. You see the advisor did what he or she thought was best. However, their idea of risk and the client's can be miles apart. By viewing your portfolio in colors, you can identify how well diversified you are and therefore more likely to handle a market downturn.

Following is a chart that would indicate a far better diversified portfolio.

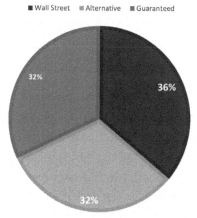

At this point some of you are now saying "Hold on. I have all of my money in bonds. Wouldn't that count for great diversification? Yet you show bonds in red money."

The Biggest Mistake of the Past Decade

In my opinion, the biggest mistake of the past decade has been advisors giving the same advice from 2000 to present as they did from 1985 to 1999. Let me explain why bonds may be a concern for many investors over the next 5 to 8 years and possibly beyond.

Do you remember what interest rates were doing in 1981? As I state earlier and sourced it, inflation over a two year period was up over 24%. According to analysis by Mortgage-X, the highest certificate of deposit rates (for 3-month CD) occurred in 1981. That year, rates reached a high of 16.691%, with an average rate for the year of 14.897%. Measures of longer- or shorter-duration CD rates also show the highest CD rates in 1981. You might be thinking "If I ever see rates like that again, I'm throwing all of my money in the bank!" WAIT! If inflation was running higher than the rate you are earning in your CD you're losing money each year! I'm not saying don't buy a 16% CD. I'm saying that is all green money and if that's all you have, then you will not be keeping up with the cost of living and instead be slowly sliding toward poverty. Again, you must have balance indicated by proper diversification through RBG.

Now let's go back to my point. What has happened to interest rates from the early 80's to present (2016)? They have for all intents and purposes done nothing but go down as seen in the Fed Funds Rate graph below:

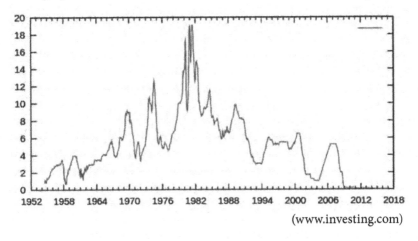

(www.investing.com)

Question: As interest rates go down, what happens to the value of bonds? They go UP! From 1981 to 2016, bonds may have helped your portfolio against stock market falls. The reason is many of the bonds you were holding (not all… like high yields) were going up in value due to falling interest rates thereby helping protect against some of your losses in stocks.

Next question: where are interest rates today? Answer: At the lowest point in history for any person who is alive today.

Final question: If interest rates are this low, what are the odds of them going down much further (if at all) versus the odds of going up over the next 4 to 6 years? I would say the chances are excellent they will be going up! As we just learned, when rates go down, bonds go up. Therefore, if you truly believe as I do rates will be going up then bonds must go down.

That is why bonds are listed with all of the other Wall Street investments in the red. I personally believe bonds will be far more risky in the years ahead than at any time in the last 30 years. Now if stocks are losing while interest rates are slowly rising (which means bonds are also losing), where does that leave your portfolio? Of course, some bonds will lose more than others. However, the future rise in interest rates will be a sinking tide that will take all bonds with it to some degree or another.

The Problem

The problem is that most advisors today are still giving advice as if we were somewhere in 1981 to 1999. If that is your advisor, here is how you can better prepare yourself and not be so dependent on him or her alone.

Step #1:

Grab a sheet of paper and create three columns. Title each column as either Red, Blue, or Green. Go through all of your investments and put the name and dollar value of each investment or asset you own in the proper column based on my description of each above. Do not include your primary residence value or life insurance death benefits (cash values are okay) as you can't depend on them for income. Once complete, add up each column and identify the percentage of investments in each category. To identify the percentage, grab a calculator. Take the total value of the red column and divide it by the total value of all three columns.

Example:

> Total of all three columns = $ 1,152,345
> Total of red money = $ 932,131
> $ 932,131 divided by $ 1,152,345 = 81% red money.

Do this for each column and you will now see how well diversified your portfolio is compared to just being diversified in Wall Street.

Most of the time, it is not unusual for us to see prospective clients without any Blue Money. In the case just illustrated, it would most likely be 81% red, 0% blue and 19% green (and all of the green money would most likely be in the bank at today's rate of just 1%).

This is NOT proper diversification and now you know that. If you are working with an advisor who understands RBG, then you can now communicate with him or her in a manner that you will both understand YOUR wishes and not just their opinions.

On many occasions, I have had clients call me up before their quarterly reviews. They might say something like, "I was look-ing at my portfolio and I'm not sure I have enough green money. When I come in, can you be prepared to share ideas with me on other investments that might fit into the green category and be right for me?" Now that's putting you, the client, back in charge!

When you find an advisor who understands this concept, they can better help educate you and create a balanced portfolio that will help you achieve your financial goals. If I know a client must average 5% in their portfolio to reach their goals, I can then edu-cate and guide them into making smart RBG investments that together will MORE SAFELY help them achieve this 5% objective.

Finally, once a RBG portfolio is properly achieved, it cannot be considered done or complete forever. Ongoing rebalancing between the RBG is critical to make sure you stay on path with your objectives. In addition, as economics change, your advisor may recommend changing the percentage of allocation to each category in order to maintain the ability to achieve the pre-determined goals you selected at the beginning of your relationship.

Next we'll discuss forming your own personal pension plan.

CHAPTER 7

Forming Your Own Personal Pension Plan and Guaranteeing Your Income for Life

The world of investing is far too broad and complex for someone who is untrained in investing and economics (as well as those who spent their career in the investment world) to understand enough to secure and guarantee their economic future.

I have one client who I will refer to as Bill. Bill has most of his retirement assets with my firm and counts on us to direct his way financially. However, Bill has about $100,000 in his personal account outside our firm because he wants to do some of his own investing and believes he can earn a better return by doing so. Bill spends 4 to 6 hours per day at his computer following his portfolio and researching his investments. I will admit, he is doing quite well (slightly better than what we have achieved). However, it comes at a great price. Bill's wife constantly tells me of his sleepless nights, worries and fears about his investments. I'm fearful the stress could shorten Bill's life! I can think of a lot of ways to spend the 4 to 6 hours per day that Bill is doing rather than in front of a computer worrying about his stocks!

There is one investment that seems to be appropriate for many people depending on their age and financial goals. Let me caution that it is not the ONLY investment that should be in your portfolio, but could warrant your interest, depending on your rate of return needs and risk tolerance level among other things.

It is a green money account called a "Fixed Index Annuity" (sometimes referred to as an Equity Index Annuity). In this chapter, it will be my objective to explain in general how a Fixed Index Annuity works.

With so much uncertainty today, the FIA comes with some guarantees by the issuing insurance company, most important of which (depending on the options chosen) can provide an income for the rest of your life regardless of market conditions. There are (as with any investment) some drawbacks to annuity that we will address as we look more closely at them. To make it more efficient, I will refer to the Fixed Index Annuity for the rest of this chapter as an FIA.

You will find most stock brokers dislike this type of investment and will seldom recommend it. There are two reasons for this. First, their broker/dealer (the company they work for) refuses to allow them to sell it. Not because it is a bad investment. Rather it's because of the second reason brokers won't recommend this annuity; they can't trade it and make commissions or trail fees (ongoing annual commissions) off of it the way they can on stock and bond portfolios. Also, once you have invested in an FIA investment, you no longer need a professional to manage the money every year. This is because it is guaranteed against loss of principal or earnings by the insurance company and all management of assets is handled by the company at no risk to the investor. This costs the broker/dealers a profit. Whether you know it or not, I believe they are not in business to help you as much as they are to make money.

I recommend managed money accounts and other securities to my clients. However, why wouldn't they also recommend as part of a complete and well balanced investment portfolio, a portion into a guaranteed investment that can create a pension-like income for their clients that can never run out for the life of the client? I can only think of one reason… it doesn't make them enough money. They can't constantly trade it and make commissions each time.

Each broker will give their reasons why they may or may not think FIAs may be a good investment for you. My goal is to share what I see as some of the key factors of FIAs and let you be the judge of whether or not they are the right fit for part of your portfolio.

Before we begin explaining the general basics of how these invesments work, it is important for you to understand that there are dozens of insurance companies selling these investments and each company can have 3 to 10 various forms of FIAs. I can in no way offer a company name or specifics for each FIA available, that will have to be left to your professional financial advisor to guide you to the one that he or she feels is the best fit for your objectives and goals.

How Do FIAs Differ from Other Forms of Annuities?

Many times when people come into our office, and we mention the word annuity, we can get an initial negative response. I believe this is due to either false information or a misunderstanding of what they are and how they work, or a commission motivated broker sold them an inappropriate one. There are two major types of annuities: **fixed** and **variable**. Most of the negativity we hear surrounds the idea of a variable annuity.

Variable Annuities (VAs)

Variable annuities, with the exception of a fixed option or money market fund, are Red money accounts. Basically they are nothing more than a group of mutual funds held in a separate account by the insurance company and wrapped in a shell called an annuity. The reason for this is that a traditional mutual fund is a taxable investment. However, the separate account that holds mutual funds inside of a VA makes it a tax-deferred way to own mutual funds. While definitely an advantage, it comes with some concerns. First, the fees within a VA can be quite high. Typically, you would see costs in the range of at least 2% to 3% per year. This is why many advisors (and I agree with them) teach that it may not be wise to put IRA money inside of a VA. You can usually buy the same mutual fund in an IRA outside of a VA as what you might find in a VA. Therefore there is sometimes little reason to put IRA money into a VA since the IRA is already tax-deferred. Also, with the exceptions stated above, you would then save paying the enormously high fees that a VA charges. Because VA's are mostly Red money, it is a Wall Street investment and therefore can lose money.

One of the most misleading things I see many brokers do is to sell a rider on the VA called an income rider and mislead the investor as to what the rider does. Please understand that there is nothing wrong with purchasing an income rider in a VA account. Under the right conditions and with proper explanation, the rider can be a wise choice. The problem comes in when the market falls and a client gets their statement. They call their broker to express their concern over the losses they just incurred and the broker tells them they are looking at the wrong number and points them to the rider value. Why is this misleading? The rider value in a VA is a second line item *that is only of value if the annuitant (usually the investor) decides to take his or her money out over time.* If the investor says I want all the money now, they would get the actual value of the account which could be worth far less than the rider value and certainly could be less than what they put into the account.

So remember, a VA is Red money that does not guarantee your principal or earnings. It is very expensive due to fees of 2 to 4%. Also, VA's (as all annuities) come with a time commitment and a withdrawal charge if you take out your **entire account** early. However, you can usually take out 10% each year without a charge. Most VA's time commitment ranges from 3 to 9 years. If your number one concern is growth, and you can settle for an income instead of getting your principal back, then these could be an investment you may want to investigate.

Fixed Annuities

Fixed annuities come in two forms, **fixed index** and **fixed interest** annuities.

Fixed interest annuities act very much like a CD in a bank. CD's however, are insured by the FDIC, whereas Fixed Annuities are guaranteed by the insurance company and an insurance industry form called the Legal Reserve. Please note the legal reserve is not a federal entity or backed by the government. Rather it is an industry guaranty.

With a fixed annuity, you invest with the insurance company and receive a fixed rate of interest for that year. Though the initial fixed rate is guaranteed for a time, the rate of interest you receive can usually change during the entire time you hold it as rates change. Since we are currently in a low interest rate environment, fixed annuities can be a good choice. This is because as interest rates go up, there is a good chance that your rate of return will change each year and increase with them. Though the rate is guaranteed for a year at a time, when you invest in a fixed annuity you are investing in a "time deposit." This means you buy them for usually 3 to 5 years or more. If you pull out early, there could be an "early withdrawal" charge for not honoring the time you committed to. However, fixed annuities do something CDs don't. Each year you are typically allowed to pull out up to 10% of the balance of your account without a penalty charge. This offers some flexibility. When you combine this with the potential of a rising interest rate as rates in the market place increase, it can be considered a good conservative investment.

Fixed Index Annuities (FIAs)

The most important aspect of a FIA is that it is guaranteed against loss (unlike a VA). Your principal is guaranteed by two factors. First, it is guaranteed by the insurance company that issues the annuity. Secondly, it is supported by the legal reserve system as mentioned before. Again, it is important to know the legal reserve is not a federally backed program. Rather, it is a program supported by the entire insurance industry. If you have your money with company "A" and they someday got in trouble financially, then the other member companies within the legal reserve system would step in and honor your money. The only way you can lose your money in an FIA annuity is if the entire insurance industry went broke at the same time. So, while not government guaranteed or FDIC backed, the FIA comes with a very strong set of its own guarantees.

Insurance Company Ratings

Since your fixed annuities value is guaranteed by the issuing company, it can be important to check the ratings of a company you might consider investing with. This can be done by going to www. ambest.com.

How Does the FIA work?

While FIA returns are tied to market performance, your investment is never actually subject to market losses. Let's assume you invested $100,000 on November 28th. During the first year of your investment (November 28th until November 28th of the following year), if the stock market has a gain, you could have a profit. However, if the stock market loses money, your balance is guaranteed not to go down. There are three main ways the annuity could profit in an up market.

First, they could pay you on the point to point basis. This simply means that if on November 28 of year one the market was at 10,000, and one year later it was at 10,500, you would see a gain of 5% or $500 on your investment.

THE CATCH: This investment form usually comes with a cap on how much you can earn. The caps can change each year and are dependent upon several factors of which one is interest rates and the other is the cost of options in the market.

Over the last 14 years that FIAs have been offered, I would say the average Point to Point Cap in my own experience has been around 5% to 8% depending on the insurance company and product. In 2001, Caps of annuities my firm represented were as high as 15%. This means you would secure 100% of the market gain up to the cap each year, but in no case could you lose money or your previous gains if the market went negative.

Are you beginning to see the value of this to a retiree?

Second, the annuity might pay you on what is called a monthly average. This means they average the gains and losses of each month in the first contract year (both positive and negative). If the average is positive, that is your gain. If it is negative, again you can't lose money. In 2010, I had many clients using this approach and make 15% to 20%. The client who did the best actually made 43% for one year and can never again lose that gain.

THE CATCH: With this approach, the market could have a large number of negative months and then sky rocket at the end with a gain. The investor here would not make a gain as the "average" was negative.

An example would be that one year the market was up 10% and one of my clients only made 1%. Obviously, they were disappointed. However, the next year the market was up 8% and my client made 10%. Why? Because the market was mostly positive each month that year and only took a dip at the end and therefore the average was higher than the end result.

Thirdly, there is the monthly sum approach. I haven't used this approach in the past 10 years as it is best suited for when you believe we are in a bull market. This approach gives you a capped gain each month based on positive months. However, you could get an uncapped loss for each month the market is negative (keeping in mind you can't lose your money).

An example of a monthly cap might be around 2.5% per month. This is how it might look over a four month period:

Month	Market	Annuity Credit or Debit
January	+2%	+2%
February	+4%	+2.5% capped
March	-8%	-8%

If the market gained each month by at least 2.5%, then an investor could make 30% return on their guaranteed investment. However, if the market made 2% each month for 11 months (22% total for first 11 months) and then lost 24% in the last month, the investor's return would be zero (not a negative 2% as you can only gain and never lose in an FIA). That is why I seldom use this approach in a volatile market. When the market has big swings up, you're capped at maybe 2.5% per month. Keep in mind when it drops in large percentages, there is no limit on the negative credit for the year. Remember you still cannot lose your money or any previous year's earnings even if the result for the year is a negative 30%! The monthly cap can be a great consideration in bull market conditions.

In an FIA, you can change which allocation you want from year to year. You can go from point to point in year one to monthly cap the next or to monthly average the year after that. You are never committed to any choice you or your advisor might make for more than one year. You can also mix and match. You could do 50% in the point to point, 25% in monthly average, and 25% in monthly cap or any combination you desire based on which one or multiples of them would give you the best chance for gain in that year.

For the rest of this chapter, I will be illustrating with the monthly average approach.

Back to our investor who deposited $100,000. Let's say the monthly average of the index that first year went up 10%. Your investment balance would now be $110,000. Your account balance "resets" each year on the anniversary date in most FIAs. That means that once you have earned the gain ($10,000) you can never give it back.

Let's say in year two the index went down by 40%. You would still have $110,000. Not bad, but here is even greater news. Even though you didn't lose any money during the market crash, the insurance company reinvests your $110,000 at the point the index is at on your anniversary (which is down 40%) and *you now start earning for year three from that point.* If the monthly average took the gain for year three up another 10% (even though the index is still down from the 40% loss) then your balance would now be $121,000 EVEN THOUGH THE DOW IS STILL WAY BELOW IT'S LEVEL FROM 2 YEARS EARLIER! You don't have to wait for the market to get back to its previous high! WOW!

THE CATCH: It is important that you understand that FIAs were never designed to compete with a stock or stock mutual fund. Over any period of time an FIA's returns will most likely not perform in tandem with the market and must never be considered as a replacement for an equity portfolio on long-term performance. However, it can possibly make sense for an investor to have part of his portfolio in these instruments. In a period like 2000 to 2010, my experience was seeing my clients average a 4% to 7% rate of return in their FIAs, while the market for buy and hold market investors was much lower if not negative over the same period of time. In a true bull market, it would not be prudent for an investor to expect an FIA to perform anywhere close to that of an actual equity market investment.

Another important point to keep in mind with FIA's is that they all should be considered time deposits. This means that if you draw out your entire balance or more than an annual free withdrawal limit you may be subject to an early withdrawal charge. FIA's can come in terms of anywhere from 5 years or more. I personally don't believe in investing in more than a 12 year FIA.

Most FIA's offer the ability to withdraw 10% of your balance or deposited amount "each year" that you hold the account to give the investor some degree of access to their investment without charge or penalty. If strategized as only a portion of an investor's portfolio this most likely would not in my experience create a hardship on an investor.

Income Riders

Most FIA's also come with an option to add an income rider. Again, with dozens of FIAs being offered, they can all vary. However, let me illustrate a possible income rider with my favorite at the time of this writing.

To illustrate the income rider, divide a piece of paper in two with a line down the middle of it. On the left column write "Market Value" and on the right side "Income Value."

Market Value   Income Value

The income rider comes with a guaranteed growth rate published by the insurance company. For this illustration, let's say it is 8% per year, simple interest. Again assuming someone invested $100,000, the left hand side "Market Value" would grow according to market conditions and which investment option they might choose asillustrated above. However, the "Income Value" would grow by a guaranteed value, of in this case 8%. The chart would then look like this over 4 years:

Monthly Avg. Market ROR	Monthly Avg. Market Value	Income Value
+10%	$ 110,000	$ 108,000
–10%	$ 110,000	$ 116,000
+ 6%	$ 116,600	$ 124,000

If 10 years from now, the market value was only $150,000 (due to poor market conditions) and the income value was $180,000 and you wished to begin taking an income from your FIA, you would be given an income from whichever side was greater. Assuming you took a 5% income that would mean $9,000 per year of income off the $180,000 income value rather than $7,500 off the market value. Of course if the market value was greater, your income would come from that value.

But that's not the end of the story. Many income riders will also give you an increase in income during your retirement years. Your increase each year could be tied to a fixed increase (say 3% each year, regardless of market conditions) or you could have the increase tied to market performance each year. This means instead of a fixed 3% your income might go up 3, 5, 10 or more percent in one year (again based on the market) but in cases where the market was negative in that year you would simply keep the same income as the year before.

Year	Monthly Avg. Increase	Income
2	+10%	$ 9,900
3	–5%	$ 9,900
4	+10%	$ 10,890

Increase could be for your lifetime or could have a fixed number of years they would do this and then freeze the highest payment after a certain period of time. Make sure you check with the company you are considering investing with to get all of the details.

IMPORTANT: Even if you take these incomes and due to the increases, you end up using your entire principal, the insurance company will continue to give you your income until the day you die, even if you have no money left!

IF, however, you have been taking income and still have a balance in the market value side and you are past any early withdrawal charge period, you can decide to cash out and take your accumulation value with you. You never surrender ownership of your principle!

THE CATCH: Though income riders are optional, the insurance company will charge a small fee for this benefit should you select one. Consult the insurance company's investment materials as costs can differ but are usually around 1%.

It's what I call "Your Own Personal Pension Plan" and guaranteeing your income for life. Do you see a value in this *for part of a retiree's portfolio?* **How about yours?**

Reducing Your Taxes in Retirement to Have More for You and Yours (Getting the Government Out of Your Pocket)

Is an IRA, Roth IRA, 401(k), 403(b) or 457 plan the best way to go?

Let's first talk about the advantages of these plans, and then I will surprise you with all of the problems of these plans and how they can actually come back and hurt not only your retirement, but your loved ones as well.

For many, the saving grace of their retirement will be their company 401(k), 403(b), 457 or their IRA account. For the last 30 years, this is how most Americans built their retirement portfolios. Why? In my opinion there are three main reasons.

First, for most it was payroll deducted. Once we got used to a certain paycheck (minus our savings), we never missed the money flowing from our paycheck to our retirement plans. You may have even at times forgotten about it until your statement came in the mail showing your new balance.

The second reason company retirement plans were so important for many over the last 30 years, was that many employers would "match" or also contribute to your plan. This was free money and anyone who passed it up would have been crazy.

Third, it was tax-deductible from your reportable income each year. You never had to pay tax on money you were paid that went into your retirement account. Accountants and financial planners alike hailed this as a huge opportunity for all Americans and encouraged all to take part.

Now for the bad part...

We were all told to invest now and deduct it as we would most likely be in a smaller tax bracket in retirement so when we withdrew the money, we would pay less tax than while we saved it, had we not contributed to a tax-deferred plan.

At the beginning of this book, I discussed many of the current economic events that surround our nation and our financial futures. As you remember, we are now in the third lowest set of tax brackets in the last 93 years, and with all of the problems facing our nation economically, we can certainly expect higher taxes and inflation down the road. Therefore, the idea we would pay less taxes in retirement may not only be incorrect, it could be at a higher rate than the rate at which we saved the money.

If you are still working, I recommend you only contribute to your company retirement plan under one of two conditions:

If your employer is matching your contribution then by all means contribute to get the maximum match. It's free money. However, if there is no company match, I would recommend you instead contribute to a ROTH IRA. As of 2020, the maximum for ROTH contributions for those closing in on retirement was $6,000 per person (over age 50 you can each add another $1,000). If you are married that means $12,000 total for both you and your spouse. For many, this would cover most of what they are putting into a 401(k) anyway. If you happen to be saving more than the $12,000, then go ahead and put the amount over that in your company plan. At least you will have the lion's share in a tax-free position.

When clients come in with a fair or sizable amount of tax-free money, it is amazing the things that can be done to lower the tax burden on their income in retirement. Allow me to share with you a great example of how funding your tax-deductible plan actually can benefit the government more than you.

Tax the Harvest vs. Tax the Seed

Tax the Harvest

Let's say you put away $6,000 per year into a 401(k). Let's assume you are in the 25% tax bracket. That would mean you would save approximately $1,500 in taxes that you would have had to pay had you not done the 401(k). If you saved the $1,500 per year for 30 years, you saved $45,000 in taxes during your career. It looks like this:

Tax Savings per year:	$1,500
x 30 years:	$45,000

Over a 30 year period of investing let's say you averaged 6% interest on your long-term $6,000 per year. Your investment would have grown to $553,089. Not bad! You saved taxes and have a nice nest egg to boot.

However, now you retire and decide to take an interest income off your retirement plan. Let's assume you could get 5% per year off your $553,089, or an income of $27,654 per year of TAXABLE income. 100 percent of this income is taxable because you never paid tax on the deposits going into the plan or the growth while in the retirement plan. Assuming your tax rate is still only 25% (most likely it will be higher), your tax on this portion of your retirement income would be $6,913. If you are retired for 30 years and pay *$6,913 per year* in taxes that means you will pay the IRS a total amount of *$207,405 in income tax!* Now it looks like this:

Value of retirement plan at time of retirement:	$553,089
Income per Year at 5%:	$27,654
Tax Due on Income at 25%:	$6,913
Tax You Paid During Retirement:	
$6,913 tax X 30 years (age 60-90) =	$207,405

This is called taxing the harvest (the money you rely on for income in retirement).

Let's see now, the IRS let you keep $45,000 in tax savings and in return you gave them $207,405. Wow, what a deal... for the IRS. That is just off the income of your 401(k) or IRA. Now how much will be taxed when you pass away to your surviving family "on top" of the taxes on your interest income? Assuming your 5% represents only the interest income and the balance stays the same, your family would now have to liquidate the entire amount over no longer than 10 years (per the Secure Act). This would mean at least another $140,000 of tax or a total tax back to the IRS of $347,405. Remember, the IRS let you keep $45,000. WHO WON?

Tax the Seed

Let's look at the other option which would mean paying tax on the seed (the money you invested over your working life counting on it growing) rather than on the income you need in retirement.

In our previous example we deposited $6,000 into a tax-deductible retirement plan and by doing so saved $1,500 in taxes each year for a total savings of $45,000. Wouldn't it make more sense to pay the tax on the $6,000 you deposit during our current low tax brackets or $1,500 per year and put the remaining $4,500 into a ROTH IRA?

Your total Roth balance in 30 years would be $414,817 using the same factors and your net tax-free income would then be $20,740. While your net take home pay is the same, you would not be subject to higher tax rates during your retirement. Depending on your total income during retirement (the tax-free money won't count) you could then receive your Social Security Income 100% tax-free as well (consult your tax advisor or financial professional for more information on this possibility).

If you are currently retired, I will give you some options shortly to recapture as much as possible of the taxes you will be losing. However, if you are still working, you may want to get with your financial advisor and look at some other alternatives to your company retirement plan that can be structured as a ROTH IRA.

The reason you may decide to save through your company plan is if you are concerned about your ability to save without the savings coming out of your paycheck. In other words, you're afraid you might not be disciplined enough to receive the money and then save it. If that is the case, I have a suggestion.

about any company will allow you to payroll deduct and place money into a savings or checking account at your local bank. To maintain the same idea of saving as you did with your 401(k), simply ask your HR department to withhold the desired amount you wish to invest and send it to your bank account. Your personal financial advisor can then set up an auto draft against that account where each month as your bank gets the deposit, they automatically then send it to the investment of your choice. Still payroll deducted, still automatic and still off your paycheck without you seeing it. Now you can set that up as a Roth IRA which is taxing the seed, not the harvest.

You're Retired and Have a Huge Pool of Tax Infested Retirement Money. Now What?

Here are the tax brackets for 2020 as of the writing of this chapter. Washington could change them at ANY time, so make sure you check the rates for the year in which you are reading this book.

Federal Income Tax Brackets for 2023

Rate	Single	Married Filing Jointly	Head of Household
10%	$0-11,000	$0-22,000	$0-15,700
12%	$11,000-44,725	$22,000-89,450	$15,700-59,850
22%	$44,725-95,375	$89,450-190,750	$59,850-95,350
24%	$95,375-182,100	$190,750-364,200	$95,350-182,100
32%	$182,100-231,250	$364,200-462,500	$182,100-231,250
35%	$231,1250-578,125	$462,500-693,750	$231,250-578,100
37%	$578,125 and up	$693,750 and up	$5,178,3100 and up

(Source: *irs.gov*)

Using the Brackets to Convert Tax Infested Money

In a moment, I will share with you how we lower our client's taxable income to the smallest amount possible. However, for your advisor to help you with these tax strategies, it is important that you have some of your assets in either a Roth IRA or in Non-Qualified assets (that is money not in a retirement plan we refer to as NQ) *in addition to any retirement money you hold.*

If you have mostly pre-tax retirement money, then you need to get some converted to NQ or tax-free in order for these plans to help you save on taxes. Here is how you can use the brackets to maximize the conversion.

Always be aware of where your taxable income will be each year. This may mean closer communication with your tax advisor. Assume you are a married couple filing jointly whose taxable income in 2020 is $100,000. Looking at the brackets just shown, you would not move into the next bracket of 24% until your taxable income is over $321,450.

This means that if you decided to convert IRA money to a ROTH IRA or NQ money this year, you could do a Roth conversion by moving over $60,000 into a Roth IRA and not even change tax brackets.

Whether or not you should do this is based on advice from your tax preparer and your financial professional combined. Although we don't wish to pay any tax, please keep in mind that taxes may be going up significantly in the years ahead. Also, the old capital gains tax rate before it dropped to 15% was at 28%. Back then, this was considered a bargain to only pay a capital gains tax instead of income tax. Please understand that taxes are most likely now on sale! You may want to take advantage of this now.

Converting Tax Infested Money to Non-IRA without the Tax

For years now, the government has given write-offs to people who invested in Gas and Oil Limited Partnerships. There are many to choose from and they come from moderate risk forms of investing to high risk. For a retiree, it may make more sense to stay more toward the conservative side. Whichever way you might choose, the government may give you up to a 100% deduction for investing in these programs. If you were to take IRA money and invest it here, then you would have no tax to pay as the deduction washes against any tax you might owe. Assuming you transferred $50,000 from an IRA to a Gas program that is 100% tax-deductible, it would look like this:

Amount withdrawn from IRA:	$50,000
Tax due at 25%:	$12,500
Deposit into oil & gas program:	$50,000
Tax Savings:	$12,500
Tax due:	$0

This is especially beneficial if you need income as these programs can pay you an income for up to 20 or 30 years, and in some cases do so with some additional tax advantages. Consult your financial advisor for ones they might recommend.

Lowering Your Tax Bill Through Wise Income Strategies and Planning

The best way to explain how to do this is not to tell you, but rather show you some examples.

Bill and Mary (names changed)

Bill and Mary came to me for help. Bill had been a barber his entire life and therefore had no pension plan. Here is how their income looked before we met with them. They had no write-offs:

Social Security	$25,000 (combined)
Income Taken from IRA/401(k) investments	$18,000
Interest earnings from NQ investments	$26,400
Total Income	$69,400
Tax on SS income (85% of it at 12%)	$2,550
Tax on other income (less Std Ded)	$2,060
Total Tax	$4,610

How did I arrive at this figure?

As a married couple, if your income (counting 1/2 of your Social Security) equals or exceeds $32,000, then you must claim a portion of your Social Security Income (SSI) and pay tax on it. If your reportable income (counting only 50% of SSI) is below $32,000, then you do not have to claim or pay tax on *any* of your SSI (for single individuals the levels are different, please see your tax advisor for more information on these brackets).

At $32,000, you must claim 50% of your SSI and pay tax on it. For each dollar you make over $32,000, the percentage of your SSI you must claim increases. However, you would never have to claim more than 85% of the SSI you have received regardless of income. Please remember to always consult your tax professional for tax advice. What I share is of general nature and does not reflect state taxes that may be due.

Here is how the taxes came to be for Bill and Mary:

50% of Social Security Income	$12,500
IRA Income	$18,000
Other Interest Earned (not taken but earned)	$26,400
Total income to determine taxing SSI	$56,900

Therefore, they will be taxed the highest bracket they are in on 85% of their Social Security income or 12%.

Before sharing their taxable income, it is important to understand that as a married couple, Bill and Mary get what is called a "Standard Deduction" of $14,000 per person or $28,000 for a married couple. This can vary depending upon each couple/persons situation, *www.irs.gov.*

Standard Deduction Amount

The standard deduction amount depends on your filing status, whether you are 65 or older or blind, whether an exemption can be claimed for you by another taxpayer, whether you have a net disaster loss from a federally declared disaster, and whether you paid state or local sales or excise tax (or certain other taxes or fees in a state without a sales tax). Generally, the standard deduction amounts are adjusted each year for inflation. Use to figure your standard deduction amount.

Bill and Mary had to declare 85% of their SSI income or $21,250. As a result, it looks like this:

Total Income	$69,400
Tax on SSI (85% of it at 12%)	$2,550
Other Income (less Std Ded)	$2,060
Total Tax	$4,610

That was how it looked when they came in to see us.

The next year they maintained 100% of the same income, but their taxes fell to ZERO!

Here's how we did it.

The $26,400 of income was coming from a NQ tax-deferred annuity and was considered all taxable as the income they were taking represented the interest the annuity was earning. The principal would have been free of tax (because they already paid tax on the deposits), but the interest earned along the way is not. Since the majority of the annuity was created with money that had already been taxed (non IRA), we simply called the annuity company and asked them to annuitize the policy in order to get the same $26,400 and we wanted to know how many years the income would last. It would guarantee the $26,400 for at least 22 years or possibly longer. However, here is the best part. Because the principal in the annuity was non-IRA and had already been taxed, 95% of each payment Bill and Mary received was considered already taxed money and therefore non-taxable as income for the next 22 years. It gets better. Since only 5% of the $26,400 was considered income by the IRS ($1,320), this dropped their reportable income by $25,080. Therefore, that now means they no longer had to pay tax on *ANY of their SSI.* So here is how the new scenario and taxes looked for Bill and Mary:

50% of Social Security Income	$12,500
Annuity Income (reportable)	$1,320
IRA income	$18,000
Total	$31,820

With total reportable income now at = $31,820 for purposes of Social Security. This is below the $32,000 magic value. Therefore they did not need to claim or pay tax on ANY of their SSI income.

So the "after" picture of their income looked like this;

Reportable Social Security Income	$0
Annuity Income (reportable)	$1,320
Minus Standard Deduction	($18,000)
Taxable Income (since below Std Ded)	$0

Now an additional income of $4,610 (saved in taxes) in Bill and Mary's pocket may not seem like a lot to many of you reading this book. However, when your income need is $69,000 and you now get to keep and spend 100% of it and all it took was a phone call, I would guess anyone would accept an additional $4,610 per year to be able to spend. Wouldn't you?

Avoiding Income and Estate Tax for Those You Love with a Charitable Remainder Trusts (CRT's)

It hurts me to think of how much good can be accomplished in the world if retirees would plan ahead. I believe there are two main reasons that most retirees don't plan ahead on what will happen with their estate.

First, some people don't like discussing the subject of their own death and therefore avoid any discussion surrounding it.

Second, it is not the fault of the retiree failing to discuss it, but rather the failure of their professional advisors to do so. This failure on the advisors part can be due to:

a) No concern over it, or
b) Ignorance of this very important subject.

Rather than just talk about the strategy, I feel it is best illustrated.

Jim and Sue Jones

Jim is 71 and Sue is 69. Here is what Jim and Sue's estate looks like:

Home	$300,000
IRA Accounts	$500,000
401(k) Accounts	$600,000
Non-IRA investments	$250,000
Life Insurance	$100,000
Misc. Assets	$125,000
Total Estate Value	$1,875,000

In 2020, the estate tax exemption is at $11,580,000 per person. Therefore, no estate tax would be due for this couple. However, they do have over $1,100,000 in retirement accounts that is now subject to income tax at their passing. If their children cashed out the IRA's and 401(k)s (which I would say from my personal experience is the case in 85% of clients who have passed) the children could end up owing the federal government about $407,000 as a tax on the retirement accounts.

It would look like this:

Family	$1,468,000
IRS	$407,000
Charity	$0
Total	$1,875,000

If Jim and Sue had no charitable intent, they then could use part of the required minimum distribution (RMD) they now pay each year on Jim (and soon on Sue) to buy a $407,000 life insurance policy to cover the taxes and thus leave their children 100% of the value of their estate.

It would look like this:

Family	$1,875,000
IRS	$385,000
Charity	$0
Total	$2,260,000

If Jim and Sue had a charitable intent (American Cancer Society, Church, Missions, Homeless Shelter, etc.), they could use their RMD to once again buy a bit more insurance and *gift their retirement assets to charity*. This gift to charity does not occur until the death of the second spouse. Therefore, they maintain all control of the assets while they are alive. By giving their retirement money to charity at the passing of the second spouse, it is no longer in their estate and thereby no longer taxable to either them or the charity as the charity is of course a non-taxable entity. Now it would look like this:

Family (incl insurance of $1.1 mil)	$1,875,000
IRS	$0
Charity (leaving them the IRAs)	$1,100,000
Total	$2,975,000

Let me emphasize that strategies such as this do work. It is important when considering these ideas that you consult both your tax advisor, proper legal counsel, and your financial advisor before making a decision if this is right for you.

I hope this chapter has encouraged you to think about how a little bit of planning can actually protect your estate for your family as well as create a legacy to causes that may be important to you. God bless you as you think this through.

CHAPTER 9

How to Beat the Coming Inflation

In the first Chapter I briefly discussed the problem we face with the inevitable approaching inflation. Allow me to offer just a brief review and then follow up with how you can profit from this phenomenon that I believe is coming fast.

The last time anyone has seen any degree of inflation worth talking about was back in 1980–81 when inflation hit 21.5%. That was 40 years ago! Based on the rule of 72 (when you divide the rate of return into the number 72) you get 3.35 which is how many years it took for the cost of living to double.

Take a minute and think about that. If you were in retirement during that time, the cost of a loaf of bread or a gallon of gas or a pound of hamburger was doubling in cost every 3.35 years at that rate. How do you handle that on a retiree's income? How could your investment portfolio keep pace with the increasing costs to provide you the necessary interest income without running into your principal? An interesting fact is that in the 36 years before 1981, higher inflation would hit us, on average, about three times within each 18-year period or once every 6 years. Also, the inflation was in the double-digit range during 4 of those high inflation times over that 36-year period.

If higher inflation happened about 7 times from 1944 to 1981, what happened over the last 40 years that we haven't seen any significant inflation? One possible answer is that the Federal Reserve (Fed) has had inflation under control by controlling the rate of interest that banks pay to borrow money. This then passes down to the consumer. Each time consumers start to spend too much money thereby adding to inflation, the Fed would raise interest rates ever so slightly to discourage more borrowing by consumers and thereby lessen demand which can help toward lowering the inflation rate. If consumers weren't consuming enough, then the Fed might lower interest rates to encourage borrowing and stimulate the economy. So where does that leave us today?

Today we have a unique problem. The economy has been stifled by the worldwide Covid-19 pandemic, shutdowns, public confusion, and the federal reserves' spending continues with no substantial relief in sight. Years before the pandemic, the problem was that the Fed had been lowering interest rates for years and it still had not stimulated the economy sufficiently. Back when President Obama was in the White House, he resorted to stimulus packages using trillions of taxpayer money in an effort, to stimulate the economy. While it had some effect, it was a small and not a lasting effect, which resulted in, not much more than a bandage on the economy. Now two Presidents later, in the middle of a worldwide pandemic, the Fed has put the printing of money on overdrive. Currently buying Treasury Bonds and mortgage-backed securities at a rate of $120 billion per month. Which in turn places $120 billion per month directly into the money supply. If the stimulus by the government hasn't worked and rates can't be lowered as we are at the lowest interest rate period in modern history, what's left?

What's left, in my opinion, is that one of the worst inflationary times of modern history will ensue for three reasons. First, as stated earlier the Fed has printed trillions of dollars of new U.S. currency and flooded the markets with them. As you now know, this is extremely inflationary. Second, is the amount of government spending. In March of 2020 the CARES Act was passed in agreement from both parties in response to the worldwide Covid pandemic. With a price tag of about $2 trillion, the Act was deemed to be justified in order to avoid a deep recession. The bigger concern I have is the proverbial spigot is now wide open. The American Rescue Plan Act of 2021 signed by President Biden was $1.9 trillion of new spending, then the summer of 2021, a $1.2 trillion infrastructure plan was passed, and then before the ink was dry, an additional $3.5 trillion spending bill was approved in the Senate. Who knows how much of a liability to our kids this debt will cause? The third reason I believe this will be one of the worst inflationary times of modern history, is the PPI. What is the PPI? It is the producer price index. Which is the cost of goods and services from the producers themselves. In other words, the CPI (consumer price index) is what we spend when we buy goods or services, the PPI is what companies spend to get the product from the producer. The US Bureau of Labor Statistics recorded from January 2010 to March of 2020 these two indexes were parallel and tight together with the PPI slightly below the CPI by about .5% in most years. However, from March of 2020 to July of 2021 the CPI grew to 5.3%, and the PPI climb sharply to 7.7%. Unfortunately, and predictably, I anticipate the prices to the consumer will follow this sharp increase.

What Can You Do to Protect Your Income from the Demands of Inflation?

This is one of the area's where my RBG system really shines. Let's break these down into each color and how to use them to fight inflation.

RBG in action — getting the Green right.

First, your current level of risk needs to be assessed and in most cases for retirees, it needs to be balanced more suitably. My RBG process is essential for determining this proper balance. It helps you achieve a truly balanced portfolio, where the portfolio has some allocations in uncorrelated categories to the market. This is a fancy way of saying, some investments move with the volatility of Wall Street, some of the investments do not participate in market corrections, others react in the opposite direction as the market is moving, and the last category is investments that move up or down regardless of market gains or losses. Currently we are heading into an era of inflation, and therefore, if appropriate to your situation, your RBG portfolio plan should have an emphasis toward hedging against inflation.

To create that emphasis, we first ensure your Red and Green money are repositioned to a more appropriate allocation. Most of the time, this means moving more money to the Green category. Any money moved to the Green category is now protected from market loss. This explanation was covered in chapter 6. If the market loses even 2% and your account didn't lose a dime, you will not have to make up for this lost money to buy a product at the store. Yes, with inflation the product will cost slightly more, but again, you don't have to make up for market loss, that places you ahead of the inflation game for that portion of your money. As the great investor Warren Buffet always says, "Never lose the money".

How to use Red Money

The Red money is in the market. Most advisors say this is how you hedge against inflation: have money in the market, because over time it will outpace inflation. I believe this is a little too simplified and a naive statement on its own. True, the market has outpaced inflation, but only if you use 20-, 25-, or 30-year averages. For example, what if you retired in 2002 right after that market crash? First off, you would be retiring on less money which of course is problematic. But here we are talking about how advisors say to use the market as a hedge against inflation. Inflation from 2002 to 2012 averaged 2.9% and the market return was also 2.9%. That is not much of a hedge on inflation. Now of course there are better and there are worse sets of years, but you may notice that every time a chart is used to show the market is a good hedge against inflation, they usually use a 30-year chart because that timeframe usually shows the best returns. So how do we use the RBG system to allocate the Red money as a hedge against inflation. The answer is fund allocation and back to the uncorrelated stock charts. Within the Red money portfolio, we use a correlation grid to ensure the assets chosen are mostly uncorrelated to each other and with a focus on high quality value stocks and or ETFs as inflation starts to rise.

How to use Blue Money

Now, with those categories in place, we can move onto how to use Blue money as another hedge against inflation. This money, as you recall, represents investments that are often referred to as "Alternative Investments". These are things like Real Estate Trusts (REITS), equipment leasing programs, precious metals, like gold and silver, high grade rare coins, collectibles, and a relatively new category called Crypto currency. The Blue category is typically the smallest asset recommended in the portfolio. This can represent 10% or down to 2% of a portfolio depending on risk tolerance and liquidity needs.

Blue Money — REITS

Real Estate Trusts can be a good asset if you find the right project. My caution to you is they can be illiquid (meaning, they hold your money until the project is complete, this can be years). For that reason, I am not currently recommending any REITS as this time.

Blue Money — Gold, Silver, and other Precious Metals

Please remember this: everything is at some time or another in a bubble! Let's look back at 1981-82, when the Dow first hit 1,000, everyone was talking about how the Dow was in a bubble and to get out NOW! Of course, you know the rest of the story. Sure, it's gone up and down, some larger swings than other years, but look at where we are today. For example, in the summer of 2021, the Dow hit 35,000 for the first time; 40-year timeline from 1,000 to 35,000. That is quite a run.

When investing in anything, always start with this fundamental question. What caused the value of that item to move up or down. In this case, what has caused gold to climb to its 2012 peak values, then fall for the next few years and then in late 2020 to climb just above $2000 per ounce? The second question is what might be in the mill, so to speak, that would cause gold to once again take off and are the fundamental causes still in place to cause it to grow in value once again? If the answer is yes, then we should not worry about the current value as much as we should think about the potential future value.

What's happening that could cause the price of gold to rise? Let me share a few thoughts as to why I believe this is the case. Part of the reason that gold fell in value after 2012 is the failing economics of China and other Asian countries. In the late 90s and early part of the new century, Asian markets were growing too fast. This led to an economic bubble burst in this part of the globe. Since many citizens of the communist Asian countries do not trust their governments, they like to invest in gold.

What about India? I believe the same thing is transpiring there. What about Russia? The same!

What about the good old USA? Do you think many are worried about the future of our currency? Do you think many are worried about the possibility that we could follow the ways of Greece, Italy, Ireland, or Portugal? Although some of these countries have had a robust recovery, can we at least admit that faith in most countries and their government's currency, or even their government, is not at an all-time high? Where do people go when they have lost faith in their government's currency? They go to gold. The fundamentals are there, and I believe will continue to be for quite some time until we work through all the economic problems we face worldwide.

During periods of economic uncertainty, rising inflation, the ongoing geopolitical tensions, and of course the battle to defeat Covid-19 and any of its many variances; precious metals tend to do well during these times. Just turn on the world news for two minutes and you will certainly notice one, if not all of these items being talked about. How will the ending the 20-year war in Afghanistan effect the world politically? With higher tensions in the entire area, will it cause oil prices to rise? What will China or Russia do next? How will that affect our prices here at home? Will it cause inflation to rise more quickly? We are entering another inflationary time and if it persists, then precious metals are an important asset to own.

How Should You Buy Gold? Or for that matter any of the precious metals.

While I will leave it to each individual to identify how they prefer to invest in the metals, I do have some options for you.

For this example, let's use gold as your choice of purchase. You can buy actual gold bullion. This can be done in bricks of gold or in the form of gold coins minted by various governments. A gold brick isn't the same size as a regular brick like you would build a house out of. It is a bit larger (2 cubic inches larger). Let's assume you are thinking about buying a gold bar (like that stored at Fort Knox). A gold bar weighs 400 Troy ounces... that is 27.4 pounds. With a density of 0.698 pounds per cubic inch and the bar having a volume of about 39 cubic inches (a regular brick is 6" x 3" x 2" and has 36 cubic inches of volume) the value varies daily and is reported on the gold market per Troy ounce. If gold was at about $1,787 per ounce. At that price you would take 400 x $1,787 = $714,800 for each brick in U.S. Dollars. Needless to say, for most of us, that would be a bit out of our league.

For this reason, most people who wish to own and hold gold do so by buying gold coins. U.S. coins are offered in 1/10 oz., 1/4 oz., 1/2 oz., and 1 oz. denominations. These coins are guaranteed by the U.S. government to contain the stated amount of actual gold weight in troy ounces. This makes owning gold much more convenient and easier to store. Buying gold and holding it in your possession, does have a couple of drawbacks. The commissions and fees can be anywhere from 3 to 8%. This is money not going into the value of gold, but rather pure up front and back-end costs to both buy it and sell it. In addition, there are shipping costs.

A more affordable way to own gold or any other precious metal, is to buy an "Exchange Traded Fund" or ETF. When buying an ETF, you are buying shares of ownership in the bullion itself, but in the form of shares not the actual metal. The advantage of this is much cheaper costs to own then the physical metal, ease of storage, and immediacy of both buying and selling your shares on the open market. This for most people is the most common method for buying this asset. Gold ETFs, Silver ETFs, and a mixture of metal ETFs all are a good place as a hedge against inflation.

Blue Money — High Grade Rare Coins

First let's talk about what a HGRC is. Collectible coins come in different grades from MS-40 to MS- 70 or PF-40 to PF-70. HGRCs are only those coins at a rating of 65 or higher. While all coins can benefit from rising interest rates and inflation, the very best opportunities are in those rated as 65 or higher.

To get an idea of just what coins can do, we can look back at the last time we had significant inflation in the early 80's. During that time (over a period of approximately 2 years), some HGRCs increased in value by over 1000%. That means if you had $10,000 in HGRCs, it could have grown to more than $100,000. Of course, I must say at this point, past performance is not an indication of future results. Are we in the lowest interest rate environment that we have seen in decades? Yes! But I need to make a cautionary note here as well. This coin market has been on the rise for a few years now. It started rising about March of 2020 and U.S. interest rates had not started rising yet. What changed. Covid-19 and the world-wide pandemic that ensued. Soon after, inflation started to rise and here we are today. The pandemic is not over, inflation is rising, and what does that mean? This sector could continue to climb and if it does, then it is a reasonable place to invest a portion of the Blue Money as a hedge against inflation. To put this sector in perspective; Yes, the HGRC market has been climbing for a few years, but we are not at the levels we were in 2007 to 2008, or 1992 to 1993, or not even close to the levels reached during the late 80's and early 90's. It is important to note that as with any investment or commodity that HGRC's can also lose value. Should interest rates fall in the future rather than go up in value, it would only be logical that the value of your coins could fall as well. So, the big question is: "Which way do you see interest rates going over the coming years?

So how does a person start investing in this sector? Two ways. The physical coins themselves or coin index funds. With rising inflation, either choice is a viable way to hedge against inflation.

Let's start with talking about the physical coins. The lowest price one might expect to pay for a HGRC with a 65 rating, would start around $3,000. To hold these coins after purchase, I would recommend investing the $35 or so at a local bank to get a safe deposit box. Never keep the coin in your home in case of a fire or even a robbery. Another point to be aware of is how to sell your coins. Who would buy a coin for $100,000 that you paid $10,000 for just two years ago? I know that sounds extreme, but those were the gains on some of the coins in the late 80's. Will we see that again, no one knows for sure. Getting back to selling the coins;

there are auctions around the country each month that work very similar to the stock market. At the time you wish to sell you would send or deliver your coin to your coin dealer who would then take it to auction. You never have to find a buyer yourself, the coin dealer does this. The more inflation that takes place, the higher the demand for HGRCs and therefore, the more you can sell it for. Remember, if the demand for that coin is not present at the time you want to sell, then you would have to wait it out.

Most important, it is imperative you find a coin dealer or financial advisor you trust to lead you to the right coins to make sure you don't get taken advantage of. HGRCs are something most people really know little about, so make sure you find advisors and dealers you can trust.

A second way to own rare coins is through an index fund. Similar to owning a stock market index fund, you don't physically own a company, you get a diversified selection of securities of many companies. A coin index works the same way. You own a diversified selection of a certain type of coin or category of coin. Here is a list of coin indexes from one source, pcgs.com. I choose PCGS because, since 1986 they have been the industry standard for authentication and grading of rare coins. These are different types of coin indexes available to the public. Generic Gold Coin Index, Mint State Rare Gold Coin Index, Proof Gold Coin Index, Mint State Type Coin Index, Proof Type Coin Index, Morgan and Peace Dollar Index, Silver and Gold Commemorative Index, 20th Century Coin Index, PCGS3000® Rare Coin Index, last but not least the Key Dates and Rarities Index. Indexes allow you to invest in multiple coin types without banking on just one coin going up in value.

While no market or investment can ever be guaranteed or subject to warranty, including rare coins and the rare coin index market, this is a unique facet of that market that usually performs well in inflationary times.

Blue Money — Crypto currency

Yes, this is a new class of assets and yes, it is currently very volatile and not for the faint of heart. With that said, it can be a very good place to hedge against inflation with a small portion of a portfolio. I have been investing in Crypto currencies since January 2018 and have seen wild swings in the price of this asset class. This is not a short-term asset and certainly not something I trade daily; in fact, I am currently only a buy and hold investor in this class. As of this writing, there are no cryptocurrency ETFs trading in the U.S. markets. Major players like, Morgan Stanley, Fidelity, and TD Ameritrade are all seeking approval for some version of an ETF. Currently the closest product to a cryptocurrency ETF is the Bitcoin Investment Trust (GBTC). I am not recommending this company; I am only using it as an example. There are other ways to invest around this asset without investing directly into the asset. One way is investing in the right Bitcoin mining companies. What I am personally waiting for is an ETF that includes Ethereum (ETH). Much of the blockchain is built on the Ethereum infrastructure.

Without diving too deep into the weeds here; I want to give you a very brief overview of what crypto currency and the decentralized system are all about. A large brushstroke of the asset class is that crypto currency started out as a decentralized banking system. In the past the only way to transfer money electronically was to use an intermediary like a bank or companies like PayPal. Bitcoin changed that in 2009 by creating a decentralized system that could be used around the world with transaction times reduced to minutes instead of sometimes weeks. Also, it cut out most of the middlemen transaction costs. In the past, using the banking systems, you could be charged a flat rate of about $45 and/or a percentage of the amount you're sending. This could be .5% to 3.5% of the total amount you want to send, ouch! It gets worse. Most countries charge a margin on the exchange rate to the tune of 5%. In addition to those charges, many banks charge their customers another flat rate somewhere between $15 to $25 to the person receiving the funds. So, let's say I wanted to send money to a friend in Nepal. If I use the lowest costs listed above and I wanted to send $7000 (obviously they must have been a good friend for this fake scenario). Ok, back to the story. To send $7000 USD, the costs would have been, $45 (flat fee) + $35 (.5% of $7000) + $15 (receiving end flat fee) that would equal $95, just to send the money! Depending on the destination country it could have cost $315 for just that one transaction. What if I only wanted to send $200, then almost half of the money could have been eaten in fees. This is a very slow and inefficient method of transferring money. A simple Google search indicated that $5.1 trillion dollars are transferred every day. Ever wonder why there are so many banks in every town? Using the decentralized system, if each person has an electronic wallet (like a wallet from Coinbase) then the transfer would take between 3 to 17 seconds with a cost of $0.01 to $1.00 depending on the crypto coins used. This is just one example of how the decentralized system will and is currently changing the world in how business transactions are conducted. This decentralized system is not just for currency transactions. There are many aspects of what this system can and is doing to create efficiencies in many industries. Another example is something called a smart contract. This is a new term used for any electronic contract. An example of this is flight insurance can now be automated and executed immediately to cover flight delays predetermined by the airline. If the flight was for example, 3-hours delayed and that triggered a claim, then you get notified via an app on your phone and with a click of a button your claim is paid immediately to your credit card. No delays, no phone hold times, and certainly no standing in airport lines to get your claim processed. There are hundreds of these examples in many different industries and therefore I believe this is an asset class worth watching with a close eye.

Anyone starting an investment in this asset class should start very small and diversified between different kinds of companies. Do your research and ask lots of questions. As I stated earlier, it's a new arena and that alone makes this type of investing a speculative investment. I called this section "Crypto Currency" for the commonality of the name, but as you can now see this asset class is much bigger than some random digital currency that someone with math and code-writing skills just made up on the back of napkin. This class is in my Blue Money category and can offset rising inflation because of its growth potential and the fact that it is uncorrelated with the stock market, is a bonus we can't overlook.

Beating the coming inflation — Closing Remarks

Every situation, every portfolio, and current or future needs are unique, so if any of these Blue Money asset concepts are being considered as a viable investment to diversify your portfolio with the intent of beating the inflation issues ahead, then I strongly urge you to discuss these ideas in detail with a Fiduciary that can recommend what is most appropriate for your situation. And in my opinion, the best way to accomplish this is by running a full RBG report and looking at all your options.

As with all battles to be waged, we must know the enemy, [inflation / price inflation], and determine which weapons will protect us... and then we must act prudently and get enough of whatever is needed to do the job. Anything less, would cause our financial plan, not to mention financial future, to be placed at greater risk. History has more than proven this and to essentially quote Spanish-born, American philosopher Jorge Augustin Santayana, "He who ignores the mistakes of history is doomed to repeat history's mistakes." This applies to every facet of our lives and is just as applicable, if not even more so, in finance and economics.

CHAPTER 10

Your Financial Advisor and Your Own 7702 Plan. Huh?

It amazes me how many so-called financial planners are nothing more than investment salespeople. Their idea of planning for a client is 90% Wall Street investments (meaning stocks and bonds or even worse, all mutual funds). They ignore anything offered by insurance companies like Fixed interest or fixed index annuities and even life insurance needs. On the other end is the insurance agent who believes all financial issues can be handled by life insurance or annuities.

The problem consumers face is that regardless of what the advisor is "selling" they all call themselves "Financial Planners". Can we once and for all call them by what they are?

Stockbroker: **SELLS** Wall Street investments like stocks, bonds, mutual funds, exchange traded funds and Variable annuities (which are mutual funds with a wrapper allowing tax-deferred growth).

Registered Investment Advisor (RIA): Same as above but must be held in a managed account by a third party.

Insurance agent: **SELLS** annuities (fixed interest and Fixed Indexed annuities only) and life insurance.

So, what is a financial planner? Any of the above could act as a financial planner "IF" they suggest a prospect diversify their investments possibly into all of the above. Whenever the advice is centered only on Wall Street you have either a Stockbroker or RIA. If their advice is centered only on insurance and annuities, then they are an insurance agent.

If the insurance agent suggest meeting with a stockbroker or RIA to complete the financial plan (which they could have both licenses), then they are acting as a financial planner. If the stockbroker or RIA suggest meeting with an insurance agent (or are licensed as one themselves), then they are acting as a financial planner and in both cases properly serving you without pretending, they are all things to all people.

The problem I see almost 100% of the time is mostly caused by Stockbrokers. People come into my office and when we break down their investments into Red, Blue, and Green money, we see that they are 90-95% in Wall Street investments. Insurance agents seldom cause this problem as typically a small portion of a client's portfolio is in insurance related products or investments. Also, insurance companies have self-imposed restrictions that don't allow an insurance advisor to overload you on annuities and insurance. Unfortunately, a stockbroker has no such restriction and could have you 100% at risk in the market /wall street.

Why do say having such a high percentage of a client's assets in Wall Street is bad or dangerous? Let's look at a real example of an actual client. **I have changed the name for obvious reasons.**

The Story of Phyllis

In May of 2007 Phyllis came into my office seeking advice. I ran a Red, Blue, Green analysis for her and this is what it looked like.

Phyllis Anderson			
May 12, 2007			
Wall Street Investments			
Fidelity Investments	NQ	Phyllis	$103,457.00
Ford Motor Co SSIP	401k	Phyllis (Patrick)	$754,090.00
Vanguard Mutual Funds	IRA	Phyllis (Patrick)	$344,512.00
Vanguard Mutual Funds	IRA	Phyllis	$162,789.00
Total Wall Street Investments			**$1,364,848.00**
Alternative Investments			
Total Alternative Investments			**$0.00**
Principal Protected Investments			
Bank of America Money Market	NQ	Phyllis (Joint)	$50,331.00
Total Principal Protected Money			**$50,331.00**
Total Investable Assets:			**$1,415,179.00**

Current Balance of Investments

You will notice that 96% of Phyllis' money was in Wall Street investments. For someone at her age this is far too much risk.

Now look at the following income analysis on the next page.

Phyllis Anderson

Starting Principal: $1,415,179.00   Rate of Return: 4.06 %

Age	Retirement Savings/Other Income[1]	Pension	Social Security	Principal	Investment Income	Desired Retirement Income
65	$0.00	$25,666.00	$17,820.00	$1,429,435.80	$41,514.00	$85,000.00
66	$0.00	$26,435.98	$18,087.30	$1,443,139.54	$42,601.72	$87,125.00
67	$0.00	$27,229.06	$18,358.61	$1,456,240.70	$43,715.46	$89,303.13
68	$0.00	$28,045.93	$18,633.99	$1,468,687.15	$44,855.78	$91,535.70
69	$0.00	$28,887.31	$18,913.50	$1,480,424.01	$46,023.29	$93,824.10
70	$0.00	$29,753.93	$19,197.20	$1,491,393.59	$47,218.57	$96,169.70
71	$0.00	$30,646.55	$19,485.16	$1,501,535.18	$48,442.24	$98,573.94
72	$0.00	$31,565.94	$19,777.44	$1,510,784.98	$49,694.91	$101,038.29
73	$0.00	$32,512.92	$20,074.10	$1,519,075.95	$50,977.23	$103,564.25
74	$0.00	$33,488.31	$20,375.21	$1,526,337.63	$52,289.83	$106,153.35
75	$0.00	$34,492.96	$20,680.84	$1,532,496.03	$53,633.39	$108,807.19
76	$0.00	$35,527.75	$20,991.05	$1,537,473.45	$55,008.57	$111,527.37
77	$0.00	$36,593.58	$21,305.92	$1,541,188.33	$56,416.06	$114,315.55
78	$0.00	$37,691.39	$21,625.50	$1,543,555.05	$57,856.55	$117,173.44
79	$0.00	$38,822.13	$21,949.89	$1,544,483.80	$59,330.76	$120,102.77
80	$0.00	$39,986.79	$22,279.14	$1,544,505.23	$60,238.90	$122,504.83
81	$0.00	$41,186.40	$22,613.32	$1,543,574.04	$61,155.21	$124,954.93
82	$0.00	$42,421.99	$22,952.52	$1,541,643.20	$62,079.52	$127,454.03
83	$0.00	$43,694.65	$23,296.81	$1,538,663.99	$63,011.65	$130,003.11
84	$0.00	$45,005.49	$23,646.26	$1,534,585.90	$63,951.42	$132,603.17
85	$0.00	$46,355.65	$24,000.96	$1,529,356.58	$64,898.62	$135,255.23
86	$0.00	$47,746.32	$24,360.97	$1,522,921.78	$65,853.05	$137,960.34
87	$0.00	$49,178.71	$24,726.39	$1,515,225.29	$66,814.45	$140,719.54
88	$0.00	$50,654.07	$25,097.28	$1,506,208.88	$67,782.58	$143,533.93
89	$0.00	$52,173.69	$25,473.74	$1,495,812.24	$68,757.18	$146,404.61
90	$0.00	$53,738.90	$25,855.85	$1,483,972.90	$69,737.95	$149,332.70
91	$0.00	$55,351.07	$26,243.68	$1,470,626.18	$70,724.60	$152,319.36
92	$0.00	$57,011.60	$26,637.34	$1,455,705.10	$71,716.80	$155,365.75
93	$0.00	$58,721.95	$27,036.90	$1,439,140.32	$72,714.21	$158,473.06
94	$0.00	$60,483.61	$27,442.45	$1,420,860.07	$73,716.46	$161,642.52
95	$0.00	$62,298.12	$27,854.09	$1,400,790.06	$74,723.16	$164,875.37

You can see Phyllis only needed a 4% rate of return (ROR) (top right) to be set for life financially live off the interest and leave roughly the same amount of funds as a legacy for her children and grandchildren at age 95.

Phyllis also decided to visit Merrill Lynch and seek their advice. When all was said and done, Phyllis chose to go with Merrill Lynch. I understand that this was a big decision and she wanted to go with the large firm with a reputation instead of an independent firm like mine.

Two years later in February of 2009, Phyllis called me and said, "I think I have made a mistake, can I come back in?"

When we met and we added up her investments it came to $661,089. **Phyllis lost over 50% of her money in the 2008 crash!**

I can't tell you how badly I felt for her. She spoke with tears coming down her face as she said to me.

"My husband worked hard his entire life to build these funds and in just two years I have destroyed what he worked 40 years to build for our family. I have let him and my entire family down."

Upon running the next RBG, we found that with the same 4% Phyllis would be broke at age 80.

Phyllis Anderson - After Market Crash 2/17/2009

Starting Principal: $661,089.00   Rate of Return: 4.06 %

Age	Retirement Savings/ Other Income	Pension	Social Security	Principal	Investment Income	Desired Retirement Income
65	$0.00	$25,666.00	$17,820.00	$644,729.75	$41,514.00	$85,000.00
66	$0.00	$25,666.00	$18,087.30	$625,773.18	$43,371.70	$87,125.00
67	$0.00	$25,666.00	$18,358.61	$604,062.75	$45,278.52	$89,303.13
68	$0.00	$25,666.00	$18,633.99	$579,434.21	$47,235.71	$91,535.70
69	$0.00	$25,666.00	$18,913.50	$551,715.31	$49,244.60	$93,824.10
70	$0.00	$25,666.00	$19,197.20	$520,725.41	$51,306.50	$96,169.70
71	$0.00	$25,666.00	$19,485.16	$486,275.12	$53,422.78	$98,573.94
72	$0.00	$25,666.00	$19,777.44	$448,165.89	$55,594.85	$101,038.29
73	$0.00	$25,666.00	$20,074.10	$406,189.61	$57,824.15	$103,564.25
74	$0.00	$25,666.00	$20,375.21	$360,128.21	$60,112.14	$106,153.35
75	$0.00	$25,666.00	$20,680.84	$309,753.18	$62,460.35	$108,807.19
76	$0.00	$25,666.00	$20,991.05	$254,825.11	$64,870.32	
77	$0.00	$25,666.00	$21,305.92	$195,093.22	$67,343.42	$114,315.55
78	$0.00	$25,666.00	$21,625.50	$130,294.87		$117,173.44
79	$0.00	$25,666.00	$21,949.89	$60,154.98	$72,486.89	$120,102.77
80	$0.00	$25,666.00	$22,279.14	($14,989.54)	$74,559.69	$122,504.83
81	$0.00	$25,666.00	$22,613.32	($95,386.75)	$76,675.60	$124,954.93
82	$0.00	$25,666.00	$22,952.52	($181,295.68)	$78,835.50	$127,454.03
83	$0.00	$25,666.00	$23,296.81	($272,986.81)	$81,040.30	$130,003.11
84	$0.00	$25,666.00	$23,646.26	($370,742.60)	$83,290.91	$132,603.17
85	$0.00	$25,666.00	$24,000.96	($474,857.90)	$85,588.28	$135,255.23
86	$0.00	$25,666.00	$24,360.97	($585,640.60)	$87,933.37	$137,960.34
87	$0.00	$25,666.00	$24,726.39	($703,412.04)	$90,327.16	$140,719.54
88	$0.00	$25,666.00	$25,097.28	($828,507.71)	$92,770.65	$143,533.93
89	$0.00	$25,666.00	$25,473.74	($961,277.75)	$95,264.87	$146,404.61
90	$0.00	$25,666.00	$25,855.85	($1,102,087.61)	$97,810.86	$149,332.70
91	$0.00	$25,666.00	$26,243.68	($1,251,318.67)	$100,409.67	$152,319.36
92	$0.00	$25,666.00	$26,637.34	($1,409,368.95)	$103,062.41	$155,365.75
93	$0.00	$25,666.00	$27,036.90	($1,576,653.76)	$105,770.16	$158,473.06
94	$0.00	$25,666.00	$27,442.45	($1,753,606.46)	$108,534.07	$161,642.52
95	$0.00	$25,666.00	$27,854.09	($1,940,679.19)	$111,355.28	$164,875.37

We were able to reevaluate some things, identifying a way to help Phyllis get a bit higher rate, reduce some of her spending and travel and better secure her financial future. But why? Why did she have to go through this?

BECAUSE SHE WENT WITH A SALESPERSON NOT A FINANCIAL PLANNER WHO HAD HER BEST INTEREST AT HEART!

For some reason stockbrokers always seem to believe that all things the client needs are solved by only putting the client's money into stock market investments. I have a guess why that is the case. You see, the stockbroker or RIA gets paid by how much money you have invested with them. The more money with them and not sent to insurance investments or real estate investment options, the more money they make.

Why don't more stockbrokers recommend insurance-based investments? Three possible reasons.

1. They have not been trained on them.

2. They want more money that they get paid an annual ongoing fee for each and every year.

3. They are forced to do so and told by their firm they are not to sell insurance-based investments.

I am NOT saying you should not work with a stockbroker. To have a balanced financial plan you need either a stockbroker or RIA who also offers insurance related investments. Or an insurance advisor who also works as an RIA or one of each.

Since I began using RBG concepts software, it helps the client see a picture of how much risk they are taking without depending on what an any one advisor tells them. Then the client can make up their own mind as to what the balance of investments should be in RBG analyses. The client now puts themselves in control.

The good and bad of 401k's

The next area that many investors have been misled in is their company 401k, 403b, or 457 retirement plans through their employer.

Let's begin by taking about THE GOOD in these retirement plans.

1. They are automatic savings plans.

   a. Most people would fail to save for their future retirement without having the savings automatically pulled from their earnings and put into a retirement plan.

2. "Some" companies help contribute to the plan on behalf of the employee with a matching contribution.

   a. If your company contributes (usually a percentage of your pay) then that is FREE money, and you must not turn it down.

   b. If your company requires you to contribute for them to contribute, I only recommend contributing up to the amount required to get the full contribution of the company. If your company contributes with or without you contributing, then allow them to do so but depending on your age you may want your money to go in a different direction like a 7702 plan or Roth IRA (more on this later)

3. For younger employees it's a "no brainer".

   a. Most every retirement plan offers mutual funds as the option to invest into. If you are 50 years of age or younger and have at least 10 years until retirement than this is a Strong consideration.

4. The employee gets to deduct their income by the amount invested in the retirement plan from their reportable income for that year.

The Bad in These Retirement Plans

1. Most people are novices and can't tell the difference between a stock and a bond and are being asked to make decisions about where to invest their money with little or no help in identifying their risk tolerance. Or, if there are questions about risk-tolerance they are only questions relating to risk WITHIN wall street investments.

2. Wall Street is getting richer everyday by supporting these retirement plans (especially at the expense of those plans offering only mutual funds)

3. You save tax at today's historically low tax rates to pay a much higher tax rate most likely when you withdraw the funds (more on this in a moment)

4. In virtually every case, the retirement plan lacks safer options like fixed indexed annuities or fixed interest annuities. or precious metals.

5. Rarely are there good investment options like real estate to invest in that isn't what is called a REIT (Real Estate Investment Trust)

6. Most plans will not allow the participant to move their funds outside of the retirement plan until age 59.5 or even until separation from service.

7. Many retirements have been ruined because once over the age of 55 employee/investors have no idea where else to go and leave the money exposed to the next market crash which then destroys the investors retirement due to too much risk.

8. Wall Street is getting rich off workers.

What can someone who is busy with life do?

The 7702 Retirement Plan

In Title 26 of the U.S. Tax code, you will find "section 401k" which is why so many retirement plans are called 401k's. In the same U.S. Tax Code, title 26 book, just a few pages further on your will find "section 7702."

A 7702 plan is the way wealthy Americans have saved money for decades and even over a century and for some reason the average American seems to miss out on it.

It certainly can be attributed to one of the old sayings that the rich don't pay taxes!

WHY?

Stockbrokers will seldom ever mention this opportunity because they don't manage it and can't get paid annually on it.

Insurance agents seldom mention it because they are too busy selling annuities.

A 7702 plan is using a special form of life insurance as a funding vehicle that maximizes growth of your cash value while at the same time limiting the amount of life insurance within the account, so the focus is on the growth of the investment within the plan.

WHAT ARE THE ADVANTAGES AND DISADVANTAGES OF A 7702 PLAN AND WHO SHOULD CONSIDER THEM?

Advantages

- Anyone can establish a 7702 plan usually through their insurance agent.

- The is no limit on how much you can contribute to the plan.

- You can take out tax-free distributions through wash loans.

- There is no 59.5 rule determining when you can withdraw money. You can contribute and withdraw income at any age and at any time.

- There are no Required Minimum Distributions at age 73 or 75 like with IRA's or 401k's or any other pre-tax retirement plan.

- The IRS is not involved to the degree they are with other retirement plans.

- Your withdrawals can always be tax-free.

- You can use Index Universal Life or Whole Life forms of insurance.

- Your family receives a sizeable death benefit tax-free in case you don't make it to retirement.

- In many cases the death benefit can be used to cover assisted living or long term-care needs.

- You can establish a tax-free income each month for LIFE no matter how long you may live.

- You provide for your surviving spouse should you pre-decease them.

- You can do lump sums without limits as long as the insurance company will take the sum and spread it out over a 5 to 7-year period or longer.

- The amount of income you earn has no impact on the amount you can contribute to a 7702 plan as it does with a Roth IRA.

Disadvantages

- Because life insurance is included (although not the main reason for the plan) you only want to consider the 7702 plans if you have at least 10 years before you expect to retire or 10 years before considering taking income from the plan.

- It is not a wise plan unless you are committed to contributing to the plan for at least 5 to 7 years.

- If you have no desire for protecting loved ones with a tax-free lump sum and or long term-care coverage for yourself, then you may want to consider a Roth IRA for smaller savings or a self-directed Roth 401k for larger investment amounts (keep in mind that depending on your income you may not be eligible for a ROTH form of investing).

- If you change your mind in the first 3-5 years, you may lose value do to early withdrawal charges and cost of insurance.

Let's look at some examples of a 7702 plan (sometimes referred to as a life insurance retirement plan or LIRP).

Sample #1. 53-year-old person wishing to invest $100,000 lump sum. Insurance company spreads out payments to avoid a modified endowment while paying interest on the remaining investment for a total contribution of $105,015.18 with interest.

Age	End of policy year	Premium outlay	Net distributions	Total charges	Accumulation value	Cash value	Death benefit
53	1	$17,502.53	$0	$3,607	$15,078	$3,282	$336,063
54	2	$17,502.53	$0	$3,675	$31,282	$19,714	$352,267
55	3	$17,502.53	$0	$3,750	$48,694	$37,360	$369,679
56	4	$17,502.53	$0	$3,840	$67,393	$56,296	$388,378
57	5	$17,502.53	$0	$3,904	$87,509	$76,657	$408,494
58	6	$17,502.53	$0	$3,979	$109,144	$98,535	$430,129
59	7	$0.00	$0	$2,187	$115,524	$105,165	$320,985
60	8	$0.00	$0	$2,216	$122,379	$113,747	$320,985
61	9	$0.00	$0	$2,244	$129,750	$122,845	$320,985
62	10	$0.00	$0	$2,270	$137,678	$132,501	$320,985
		$105,015.18	$0				

67	15	$0.00	$16,909	$2,340	$187,306	$169,552	$303,231
68	16	$0.00	$16,909	$1,190	$200,551	$164,154	$284,588
69	17	$0.00	$16,909	$1,193	$214,641	$158,671	$265,014
70	18	$0.00	$16,909	$1,170	$229,661	$153,137	$244,461
71	19	$0.00	$16,909	$1,107	$245,714	$147,609	$222,880
72	20	$0.00	$16,909	$997	$262,922	$142,158	$200,221

Age	End of policy year	Premium outlay	Net distributions	Total charges	Accumulation value	Cash value	Death benefit
84	32	$0.00	$16,909	$1,247	$589,764	$90,289	$119,778
85	33	$0.00	$16,909	$1,505	$629,381	$87,178	$118,647
86	34	$0.00	$16,909	$1,826	$671,342	$84,274	$117,841
87	35	$0.00	$16,909	$2,197	$715,757	$81,582	$117,370
88	36	$0.00	$16,909	$2,652	$762,711	$79,072	$117,208
89	37	$0.00	$16,909	$3,226	$812,254	$76,679	$117,291
90	38	$0.00	$16,909	$3,923	$864,437	$74,329	$117,551
91	39	$0.00	$16,909	$4,822	$919,231	$71,863	$117,825
92	40	$0.00	$16,909	$4,779	$977,795	$70,304	$109,416
		$105,015.18	$439,634				

Allianz Life Por+ Advantage Fixed Index Universal Life Insurance Supplemental Illustration Supplemental Illustration

This is a supplemental illustration that must be accompanied by the full product illustration. Refer to the illustration ledger of guaranteed values within the full product illustration for the policy's guaranteed elements another important information. Illustrated loans are shown as 100%indexed a n do r 0%fixedloans.

Using the assumptions shown in the table at the right and the premium and policy benefits specified in this illustration, this policy will mature in year 68.

Senior desiring LTC benefit and more income down the road

Notice that the total contribution by the individual was $100,000. At age 67 they turn on a tax-free income of $16,909 per year for life. At age 92 their total tax-free income they received came to $439,634. Assuming they pass away at that time, their beneficiary would receive a check for an additional $109,415 as a death benefit. This person turned $100,000 into $549,050 all tax-free.

Let's look at another and even more stellar example of what a 7702 plan can do. This would be on a male age 40 wanting to invest $10,000 per year through age 65 and then retiring.

Age	End of policy year	Premium outlay	Net distributions	Total charges	Current scenario		
					Accumulation value	Cash value	Death benefit
41	1	$10,000.00	$0	$1,908	$8,777	$2,358	$174,263
42	2	$10,000.00	$0	$1,908	$18,254	$11,976	$183,740
43	3	$10,000.00	$0	$1,908	$28,487	$22,351	$193,973
44	4	$10,000.00	$0	$1,908	$39,535	$33,540	$205,021
45	5	$10,000.00	$0	$1,908	$51,465	$45,612	$216,951
		$50,000.00	$0				
46	6	$10,000.00	$0	$1,908	$64,345	$58,634	$229,831
47	7	$10,000.00	$0	$1,908	$78,253	$72,684	$243,739
48	8	$10,000.00	$0	$1,908	$93,269	$88,629	$258,755
49	9	$10,000.00	$0	$1,908	$109,482	$105,771	$274,968
50	10	$10,000.00	$0	$1,508	$127,420	$124,637	$292,906

Age	End of policy year	Premium outlay	Net distributions	Total charges	Current scenario		
					Accumulation value	Cash value	Death benefit
66	26	$0.00	$63,120	$857	$711,248	$646,419	$788,669
67	27	$0.00	$63,120	$969	$765,351	$632,450	$777,867
68	28	$0.00	$63,120	$1,091	$822,539	$618,164	$766,221
69	29	$0.00	$63,120	$1,224	$882,992	$603,569	$753,678
70	30	$0.00	$63,120	$1,363	$946,907	$588,683	$740,188

Age	End of policy year	Premium outlay	Net distributions	Total charges	Current scenario		
					Accumulation value	Cash value	Death benefit
91	51	$0.00	$63,120	$18,680	$3,596,219	$282,560	$462,370
92	52	$0.00	$63,120	$18,511	$3,809,504	$265,332	$417,712
93	53	$0.00	$63,120	$17,112	$4,037,525	$251,315	$372,441
94	54	$0.00	$63,120	$13,921	$4,283,142	$242,791	$328,454
95	55	$0.00	$63,120	$8,389	$4,550,002	$242,804	$288,304
		$250,000.00	$1,893,600				

The total investment is $250,000 resulting in an annual tax-free income of $63,120 per year and not the totals at age 95.

Total Income: $1,893,000. PLUS a death benefit if he passes at that age of $288,304 going to his family for a total tax-free payout of $2,181,304 all tax-free on an investment of $10,000 a year totaling $250,000.

See why the wealthy like this plan?

What about you?

The 7702 plan can be used by anyone! It doesn't matter if you only invest $50-$100 per month or $10,000 a month. I encourage everyone to at least see what this plan can do for you. While it may not be for everyone, shouldn't you discover for yourself what your personal plan would look like?

Finally, if your company 401k plan offers a matching contribution, make sure you contribute to the 401k first up to the matching amount. Then take anything more you would like to invest, confer with your tax advisor and financial advisor and see if the additional savings might be considered into a 7702 plan.

CHAPTER 11

A Little About Me...

In this final chapter, I want to share with you a little about me. I grew up in a great town in Connecticut. My parents had a happy marriage. They had two sons: me and my brother Dan. I grew up like most young boys, had great parents, lived in a nice neighborhood, and didn't have a care in the world. We went on vacations and made lots of memories at the shore. I used to love the sound of the waves crashing on the beach and ran around with my brother, building sand castles and swimming all day until we wore ourselves out. Our parents always told us we could be anything we wanted to be when we grew up. We believed it. I thought every day was going to be a day at the beach.

My brother and I always got along. We had little fights like typical brothers, but we were inseparable. We did everything together. We were lucky to share a childhood together that made us feel like the world was at our fingertips. Not everyone has a childhood as nice as this, but I didn't know that. I assumed everyone was the same as me.

I grew up in upscale public schools. Looking back, I can see that the vision I had of the world was that of being carefree and I could do anything I wanted. As I entered High School, I started to feel lost. I felt that I was with a bunch of kids without focus. Everyone seemed like typical kids but took for granted the life that was given them. That was pretty much how I felt myself. My focus was lost and I started not to care about anything. I had lost my drive. I was just floating through the start of my high school career and it was going downhill. By not paying attention to my work, I was getting lost. After a long and hard first two years, my grades had fallen and my thirst for life was pretty much gone. I didn't care about anything. I did what I wanted, like the rest of the entitled kids I was in school with. Something had to change. I had veered down a path that was taking me away from the bright future I had dreamed about.

My parents saw my downward slide and decided to place me into private school. This was one of the best things to ever happen to me. They were able to place me with a whole new set of friends that actually cared about showing up for class, what they were learning, and how to build a bright future that they all wanted to have. I knew this was the place for me. Between the teachers and my new peers, I was able to get a hold on the life I had started for myself when I was younger, and set down the path to lead me to where I needed to be to attain the future I was dreaming about.

After graduating high school, I attended Monmouth University in New Jersey. Here, I was motivated. Here, I was able to take classes that would directly lead me to success. I had forgotten my old ways and the friends and behavior that had taken me to a place of failure. Now that I was in college and having a ball, I was in control of my future, and realized that my choices affected the job I wanted one day. I showed up for classes, excited to learn and make myself a better person. I knew I was smart and had the ability to take a situation and see it from all angles. I was able to come up with different scenarios and make choices for success based on my ideas. I was flying through my college years and loving every minute of it. The motivation to be my best self was evident and I was living it every day. I graduated college and had the world at my fingertips to be anything I wanted to be.

I knew that when I graduated college I wanted to have my own business. I knew I had learned so much and had my life experiences to help me be successful. I wanted to be my own boss, make my own rules, and build the life I had been thinking about since I was little. While I knew it was a monetary risk to start out on my own, it was exactly what I did. I took everything that I had learned in school and life and made something of myself. The money wasn't flowing in quite yet, and some days it was a real struggle, but I was still able to call myself a business owner and the master of my future. I lived on a really tight budget and poured my heart and soul into the world I knew I was reaching for. I listened to my peers, my teachers, and my mentors. I read all I could about being in finance and how to use that knowledge to help others build their financial future. I could help them like I knew I had always wanted to help people. I didn't want people to have to work so hard that they worked all of their lives, but didn't save properly. I knew people had no idea what to do with their hard earned money. I hated seeing so many people lose it because they weren't informed about the best ways to save and pay less taxes. I knew I could help them. I wanted to make a difference in this world, and for the better. I wanted people to have the peace of mind to lay their heads at night, knowing that they were going to be okay in retirement. My job was to grow my business and help people. What a great life goal!

All the while I was busy building my business and helping others, my brother and I had lost track of each other. He went to college to become a teacher. I knew he would be great at it. He had the biggest heart and would do right by the people in it. I was able to go build my business while he worked on his career. I was excited to see that two brothers were going to be successful in life and make a difference. We were the lucky ones.

After my brother graduated, he went into teaching. I didn't hear much from him, but life was busy for us both, so I assumed we were both on the right track. I knew we didn't have the best salaries and that we were both struggling, but wasn't that the way life was when a young man started out? I continued to work day and night to build a life for myself that would one day provide me with any income to live the life I had been dreaming about since we were young boys. My brother was doing the same. Everything was going to be okay.

Everything was not okay. It turns out, that while I was busy learning, growing, and struggling to make something of myself; my brother wasn't quite as successful. His life was taking him down a path that I didn't even know about. I was so busy pinching pennies and growing my business that I didn't see where he had fallen off the right path. My brother was actually in a really bad place. By the time 2013 had rolled around with me being oblivious to anything else in my life, my brother passed away. I was in shock. I was devastated. How did I let this happen? How did I not see that my brother was struggling so hard? Here I was, trying to help people build a solid and safe future, and my own brother had fallen through the cracks. The guy I grew up with that kept all of my secrets. The guy who had my back anytime I needed him. The same guy who wanted to be a teacher to help kids be better versions of themselves and keep a dream that one day they, too, would be successful. He wanted them to know what he had learned growing up. They could be anything they wanted to be.

Sadly, this was not the fate of my brother. I had lost my best friend. I wasn't going to get a second chance to lift my head from my desk and realize that he needed help. While I am not sure what I could have done for him differently, I would have tried everything. Anything. Whatever it took, with the few pennies I had, to help him get his life back in order. He kept it well hidden. He made his life seem like he was in control and everything was going as planned. He had me fooled.

I look back and think of everything that I could have done differently. I will always regret not being there for him, not knowing that he needed me. I can only guess that he didn't want to take me down with him, and that he knew he was going down a path that he didn't want for me, so he kept his downfall a secret.

I look at my life now and wish that I was in the same position then as I am currently. I was able to build my business up to be so successful that it is growing on its own, and clients come running to me, knowing they can trust me with their finances because I have spent my life learning how to make them their best selves for a future they were dreaming of too. If my brother was here now and having those problems, I could have moved him into my huge house, and taken care of him financially while he was getting help and on the right path again. I would have supported him like I support thousands of other people leading their best life. I work out and eat well, so I could have helped him learn to be his best physically as well. I have a whole insight on life that means happiness for me and those around me with financial freedom. I would give anything to have him here with me now.

I realize that wasn't the plan for my brother's life. I only have control over my own. I have taken all that I have learned from my brothers passing into strengthening my own life. I know that I will spend every day honoring him. I work harder and smarter and help people in his memory as well as my own goals to help them every day. Some people don't know that they are able to have financial freedom in life. Some people wake up, work, sleep, and get up the next day, spending the rest of their lives thinking that they will work until their last breath. I know something different. I know that they can have financial freedom if someone can only come to them and teach them the ways to earn it. They can have the American Dream, and I can help them get it.

I have spent years honoring my brother each day by helping people, but I knew I was missing something still. I needed a partner, a wife. I wanted someone to enjoy this life with, especially since I couldn't share it with my brother, Dan. I recently married the love of my life, Lin. We were married on September 1, 2017. I would have given anything to have my brother stand there by my side. Now, with Lin, we are on a journey together to help other people making mistakes. She sees the dream in my eyes to make this world a better place, and help people live to love retirement. Lin and I share our business and teach people the importance of talking about money early, saving early, planning for retirement, and how you can share that life with those people you love around you. It doesn't matter what stage of life you are in, we can help you. I won't let a customer come to me without making a plan for them to feel safe to live the life they want. I teach them to live their life and be present now, all the while saving for a future they can also enjoy later.

Sometimes all people need is the permission to live this life I am helping them build. I don't want them to be lost. I want them to have a plan and feel good about it. I take the guesswork out of the questions and help them build the dream that my brother and I both had when we were young. Don't stop living because you think you can't. Live your very best life today, and still plan to have the life you want in retirement. My company, Dworetsky Financial, helps plan your path to the life you have always wanted. We want you to have a worry free retirement, but still enjoy life along the way. Life is short, so plan well and enjoy each day.

Made in USA - North Chelmsford, MA
1236791_9781692948733
08.15.2023 1412